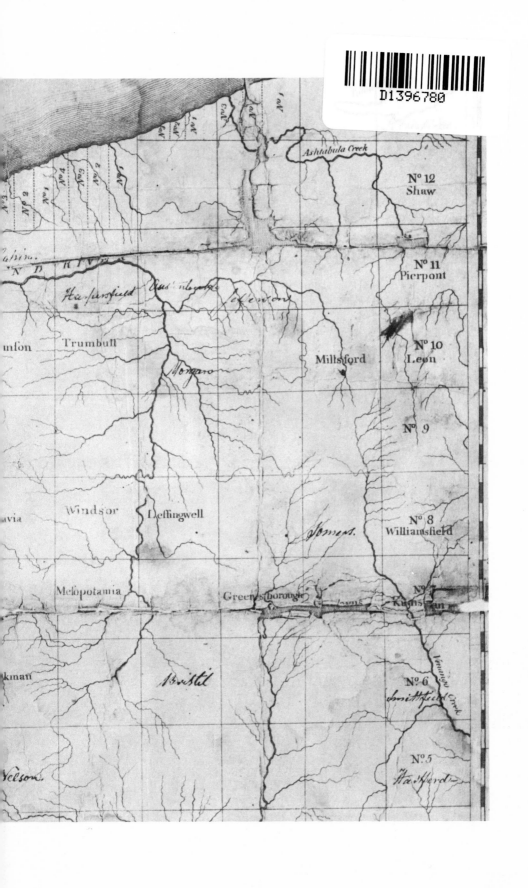

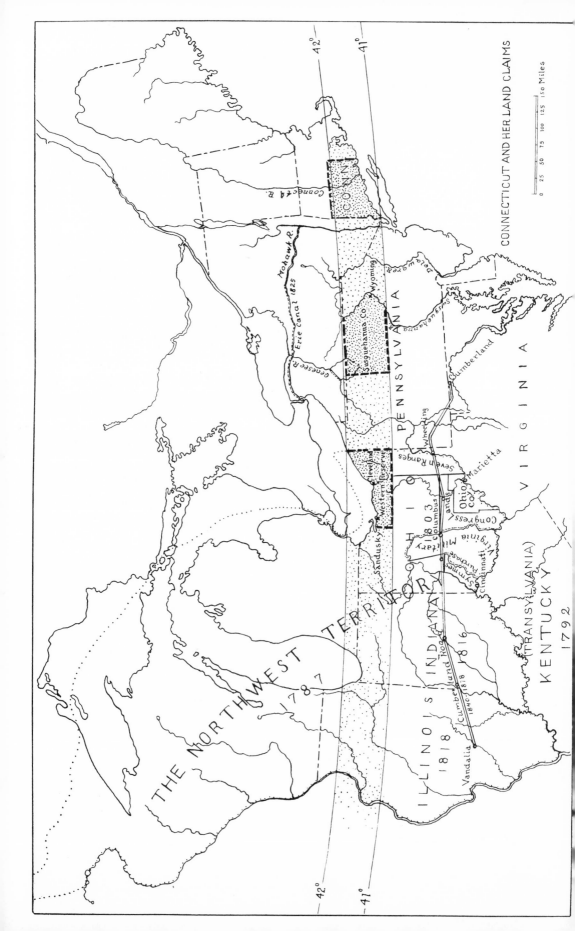

CONNECTICUT AND HER LAND CLAIMS

HERE IS LAKE COUNTY, OHIO

HERE IS
LAKE COUNTY
OHIO

THE LAKE COUNTY HISTORICAL SOCIETY

PUBLICATION COMMITTEE

Janice M. Ahstrom

Barbara S. Cooper

Jack E. Daniels

Victoria B. Van Loon

Jane G. Griffin, *Editor*

Margaret O. Collacott, *Chairman*

HOWARD ALLEN, PUBLISHER

CLEVELAND

HOWARD ALLEN, Inc., Publishers

University Center Station, Cleveland, Ohio 44106

Copyright (c) 1964 by The Lake County Historical Society. First Edition. Designed, composed, and printed at The Oberlin Printing Company, Oberlin, Ohio, and bound at The Universal Dixie Bindery, Jacksonville, Florida.

Library of Congress Catalogue Card Number 64-7540

Manufactured in the United States of America

To **PERCY KENDALL SMITH**
who first promoted the idea for this book and
who lent constant encouragement to the Publication Committee,

and

To **THE LAKE COUNTY NATIONAL BANK**
whose public interest and
whose generous assistance has made this publication possible.

ACKNOWLEDGEMENTS

The Lake County Historical Society wishes to thank the following authors, publishers and copyright holders for permission to include material from their books:

Beard, Dan, *Hardly a Man is Now Alive,* Doubleday, Doran & Company, New York, 1939.

Clark, Edna Maria, *Ohio Art and Artists,* Garrett and Massie, Richmond, 1932.

Clymer, Floyd, *Treasury of Early American Automobiles,* McGraw Hill, New York, 1950.

Cushing, Harvey, *The Western Reserve and its Medical Traditions,* Cleveland, 1924.

Eggleston, Margaret W., Editor, *Kathie's Diary,* George H. Doran Company, New York, 1926.

Harlow, Alvin F., *The Road of the Century,* Creative Age Press, Inc., New York, 1947.

Prescott, Orville, *The Five Dollar Gold Piece,* Random House, New York, 1956.

Real Property Inventory, 608, The Arcade, Cleveland, 14. 1962.

Smith, Theodore Clarke, *The Life and Letters of James Abram Garfield,* Yale University Press, 1925.

Tyler, James J., *Rev. Joseph Badger,* Proceedings of the Grand Lodge of Ohio, 1948.

CONTENTS

CONTENTS

Chapter I

In the Beginning

Some 20,000 years ago what we know as Lake County, Ohio, was covered by a great sheet of ice and snow. Moving slowly down from the north, this glacier acted as a huge scraper. It wore off mountain peaks, filled in valleys, piled up hills, and drove all life in front of it. Then, as it melted, it left behind the stones, sand and clay which are our soil; its waters formed the Great Lakes. The glacier made a raw, new land in the shapes and contours on which we live today.

As the ice cap retreated life crept in. Plants and animals which only a scientist could identify came first, and after them, the Early Hunters. These people left few traces of their life here. They were very primitive and perhaps, like the plants and animals, we would hardly recognize them.

The weather grew warmer and other changes came. Spruce trees appeared. Then shrubs, grass and flowers began to make a landscape more familiar to us. It was thousands of years after the Early Hunters, about the time civilization was beginning in Egypt, that another group arrived. These, the Archaic People, left more evidence of their visit. They hunted small animals, fished and gathered nuts and berries. Their simple tools were made of stones, bones and shells.

Most archeologists agree that these people were the forerunners of the American Indian. It is believed that they were wandering bands, related to the Yellow Race of Asia, who came across the Bering Straits between Siberia and Alaska in search of a warmer climate.

THE MOUND BUILDERS

Some 3000 years after the Archaic People, about 800 B.C., the Mound Builders came to Ohio. These were civilized men who lived very well. They were no longer wandering hunters, but farmed the rich soil of the river valleys, made pottery and wove cloth. They carved beautiful ornaments in the shape of birds, fish and animals, and etched pictures on copper and stone. They traveled many miles to obtain shells from the Gulf of Mexico, shark teeth from the Atlantic, mica from North Carolina, to find obsidian, harder than any local stone, in the Rocky Mountains and to bring back copper from the pits in Minnesota.

They came back to their villages clustered around their mounds. It is from these great piles of earth that the Mound Builders have received their name. Some mounds were built in the shape of animals, birds and snakes and had a part in the tribal ritual. Others were cones of varying sizes for the burial of their dead. Many still remain in central and southern Ohio where the Adena and Hopewell Indians brought the culture of the Mound Builders to its highest level.

MOUND BUILDERS IN LAKE COUNTY

Today there is little evidence of these prehistoric people in Lake County, where once there were a number of mounds. One was on the site of Wickliffe's Junior High School. Two are remembered in Mentor on the south side of Mentor Avenue at the curve east of Hopkins Road. East Erie Street in Painesville passed between two mounds near the entrance to Recreation Park. One was described as "circular about 15 or 20 feet high," the other as "a larger but flatter mound." In Perry two are said to have stood on the east side of Lane Road. All these and others have been leveled to make way for roads, farms and buildings.

Regrettably, these mounds were torn down before people understood the science of archeology. Today an Indian site is carefully measured and photographed at every stage of the digging. Any change in the composition of the soil is noted. Every artifact is carefully preserved, broken pieces as well as perfect specimens. From these materials archeologists can reconstruct a great deal of the life and culture of the ancient tribes. On the small evidence which we have it is only a guess to say that our Lake County Mound Builders were a later and declining expression of the Hopewell culture.

The Early Hunters, the Archaic People and the Mound Builders were all prehistoric people. All we know of them must come from the artifacts we find. There was no written history until many years after they disappeared, in fact, not until 1492 when Columbus named the natives he met "Indians," thinking he had reached Asia.

THE ERIE INDIANS

If the early men are called "prehistoric," the Erie Indians lived here "on the edge of history." When the first explorers and missionaries reached out into the interior of the continent, the Eries were reported the most powerful and warlike of all tribes. The French traveled north of the Lakes to avoid them. The English kept to the Ohio River for the same reason. The existence of the Eries is recorded and that is about all their part in written history.

From the legends of later Indians we learn a little more about the Eries. They were of Iroquois stock, speaking a dialect of the same language, and they appear to have been proud, overbearing and self-confident. There was keen competition between them and the related tribes to the east. However, the Eries were able to maintain a strong position on the south shore of the lake named after them until some of the Iroquois joined against them. This Confederation of Five Nations practically exterminated the Eries in 1655.

Two Erie village sites in Lake County have been carefully examined by archeologists. In 1929 Emerson F. Greenman, of the Ohio State Museum, Robert M. Goslin, field assistant, and three staff members dug at Reeve Village on Reeve Road near Lake Shore Boulevard in Eastlake. A Fairport Harbor site was excavated in 1937 by Richard G. Morgan of Ohio State Museum, and Goslin, assisted by Elijah H. Brown, principal of Harding High School, and several students. This Village is on the east side of East Street, south of the railroad crossing and bordering the river bluff. Also examined in 1929 were two forts, one at the point of Paine Creek and Grand River in Leroy, the other at Mill Creek and Grand River in Madison.

HOW THE ERIES LIVED

From the excavations of these Erie Indian sites we have learned much about how these early people lived. Both villages show signs of long occupation. Each had well developed pottery works. Reeve Village had a good sized burial ground nearby. The caved-in river bank may well have taken away Fairport's burial place. Nothing was discovered to indicate the type of dwelling the Eries used, but there appear to have been stockades enclosing their homes. The forts sheltered the women and children in time of war.

The squaws grew corn, squash, pumpkins, beans and tobacco, while the braves fished, hunted and fought wars. The men hunted animals for clothing as well as food, and they used the bones of animals, fish and birds for tools and ornaments. The animals most plentiful and most useful to them were the deer, raccoon, elk, beaver, black bear, gray squirrel, porcupine and wildcat. Wild turkeys and passenger pigeons furnished feathers for Indian decorations as well as meat for food and bones for tools. Fish, turtles and mussels added variety to their diet and equipment.

Evidence was found at Fairport Harbor that the Eries had had some association with white men. Sifted out were bits of white clay pipes, a portion of a flintlock gun, a knife blade, iron nails, pieces of china and stoneware, and fragments of pigs' teeth. These materials, with the Indian artifacts, demonstrate the transitional culture of the Eries from the prehistoric to the historic period.

THE HISTORIC PERIOD

After the destruction of the Eries, the land south of the lake became neutral hunting ground for the Chippewas, Senecas and Cayugas from the east, and the Wyandottes, Ottawas and Shawnees from the west and south. The white hunters and traders did not find permanent villages, and there was apparent peace between the tribes.

Although there was peace in what is now Lake County, this was not true on the rest of the continent. England and France became locked in a century-long struggle for control of colonial America. Both countries in bitter rivalry schemed for Indian friendship, fur trade and assistance.

French traders established a post at the mouth of the Chagrin River as early as 1750. Here they bartered strings of beads, guns and axes for fur pelts from the Indians. The French left their imprint on the area in some of our names. "La Grande Rivière" became our Grand River. Some think that the word "Chagrin" is of French origin. "Charlton," the name of their trading post, was still used by our early surveyors.

On an expedition to Detroit in 1760 Major Robert Rogers and his Rangers were driven by storm to take shelter at what appears to have been the mouth of the Grand River. Here they met Pontiac, chief of the Ottawas and friend of the French, who at first refused to allow them to camp. Rogers convinced him they would move on as soon as the weather improved. Unmolested, the Rangers continued on their trip in a few days, after making the first recorded visit to our Lake County by Englishmen.

DISPUTED LAND

The Treaty of Paris in 1763 gave England victory over France, but it did not bring peace to the American frontier. Indians saw the white men pushing farms into old hunting grounds, and vainly attempted to stem the tide. War parties crossed the Ohio country on raids and frontiersmen recrossed on counter-raids. The year 1775 only marked the increase of the bloody warfare.

At the end of the American Revolution England kept troops in her western forts and used the Indians in Ohio as buffer between the new United States and British plans for expansion into the Mississippi valley. British officers continued to stir up the red men who had so recently fought with England against the Colonials. As a result, our settlements along the Ohio River were not safe from Indian attack.

To end this danger, General Anthony Wayne set out with an army for the Indian camps in 1794. He defeated the tribes at the Battle of Fallen Timbers near what is now Toledo. As the English in Detroit were unwilling to oppose the Americans openly, the Indians, caught between two foes, were forced to sign the Greenville Treaty. They agreed they would no longer menace the white men east of the Cuyahoga and Tuscarawas Rivers and south of a line from Fort Laurens to Fort Recovery. Although this land was still considered their hunting ground, Wayne had broken the power of the Ohio Indians.

PERMANENT SETTLEMENT

When our New England pioneers arrived they found an Indian camp at what is now Main Street, Painesville, and another on the site of Andrews School, Willoughby. Both were at good fording places on the Indian Lake Trail. Early stories indicate that the Indians settled down for a few weeks, and then one by one would disappear for as many months. They were friendly, although sometimes a nuisance. A group were apt to show up at a cabin door just as the week's baking came from the oven, and when they left the family had hardly enough bread for supper. But as often as not, they would be back in a few days with game or new moccasins to repay the housewife.

The young boys of the early settlements delighted in watching the tribal dances and merry-making. They learned, too, something of the Indians' religion. Still visible was the ever-bubbling gas spring in Lake Erie just off the shore from North Perry Park, which tradition said was inflammable. Indian legend told of the Water God whose presence was evident in the unceasing turbulence. Another attraction was Little Mountain, whose many caves, rocks and springs led the Indians to believe it was the home of their Great Spirit.

One of the most famous Indians at this time was Stigwandish (sometimes Stigwamish) meaning "Standing Stone." A member of the Seneca tribe, Stigwandish was often called "Seneca" by the early settlers, and was admired for his honesty and integrity. He warned the people of coming raids by the English and their Indian allies during the War of 1812. Then he and the other Indians moved west to take part in the war and few ever appeared in our neighborhood again.

French, English and Indian claims to our land were eventually settled, but in our history there were still other rights of ownership in question. We must go back to the beginning of colonization to understand the conflicting claims which existed among the original thirteen states and affected what was to become Lake County.

Chapter II

The Western Reserve

When the first Englishmen came to America they were uncertain of the size and shape of the continent upon whose eastern shore they had set foot. To the north were the French, to the south the Spanish, but no one knew what lay west, except that it was the domain of the British crown. Through the seventeenth century English kings gave land to groups and individuals with no regard to geography. As one early colonist said, they "might as well have decided that the line between the states was bounded on the north by a bramble-bush, on the south by a bluejay, on the west by a hive of bees in swarming time, and on the east by five hundred foxes with firebrands tied to their tails."

In the early years of colonization the overlapping grants caused no trouble because there was plenty of room for all. But by 1750 Connecticut was becoming, in the eyes of its residents, "filled up," and men turned to Charles II's original charter. This had defined the grant as all land between 41° and 42° 2" north latitude, westward to the "South Seas." Although cutting through this area, New York's claim was too well established for serious dispute. However, Connecticut, ignoring William Penn's grant, looked upon the unsettled land of the Susquehanna valley as rightfully hers. Here she cleared title with the Indians and established a colony which had some 2000 settlers when it was wiped out in a tragic massacre by the British and Indians in 1778.

THE NEW GOVERNMENT

The First Congress of the United States faced boundary disputes all along the seaboard. There was, as well, the question of the western claims of the thirteen states, particularly those of Virginia, Massachusetts, New York and Connecticut, to the land north of the Ohio River. It is a credit to the statesmanship of our first legislators that solutions were found with so little dispute. One after another the lines between the original states were defined, and western claims were relinquished to make the Northwest Territory public domain, land which Congress could sell to support our young country. By deed of cession in 1786 Connecticut gave up her western lands, but reserved a one hundred and twenty mile strip west of the established Pennsylvania border. This "reservation" was accepted by Congress partly because Connecticut was considered small and over-crowded, partly because she had agreed to the New York and Pennsylvania boundary decisions, and partly because of the sympathy felt for her in the Susquehanna valley tragedy.

Congress's recognition of Connecticut's full right to the soil and the jurisdiction of her "reservation" created an unusual situation. The area, soon to become known as the Western Reserve, was a colony of the mother state. It posed problems of administration for the Connecticut legislature for the next fourteen years, but during that time foundations were laid for transplanting New England culture to the shores of Lake Erie.

DISPOSING OF THE WESTERN RESERVE LANDS

General Samuel Parsons bought the first piece of land in the Western Reserve in 1788. Known as the "Salt Tract," this purchase included 25,450 acres in the Mahoning valley near what is now Youngstown. In 1792, the General Assembly set aside a twenty-five mile wide strip at the western edge of the Reserve for their citizens who had suffered property losses during the Revolution. First called the "Sufferers' Lands," it became known as the "Firelands," as the greater part of the damage had been from fire. These two actions disposed of nearly one-half million acres of the Reserve.

Pressure on the Connecticut legislature to sell the remaining land came from both prospective settlers and the citizens who saw good use for the money it might bring. The General Assembly finally outlined a plan whereby the property could be sold unsurveyed. A committee of eight men, one from each county of the state, was authorized to sell the lands, estimated at more than three million acres, for not less than one million dollars (or approximately 35c an acre). This committee was required to dispose of the property as a whole rather than in parcels. Income from the sale went into a special fund for the support of Connecticut's schools and, today, this fund is still operating within its original purpose.

THE CONNECTICUT LAND COMPANY

The Connecticut Land Company was organized to purchase the remaining portion of the Western Reserve. On September 2, 1795, this association of thirty-five men gave bond and a mortgage on the lands for the amount of $1,200,000 to the state treasurer. To secure the bond and mortgage, the Company's shareholders individually pledged varying amounts, ranging from Sylvanus Griswold's $1,683 to Moses Cleaveland's $32,600 to Oliver Phelps' $168,185.

Eighteen more shareholders joined the Connecticut Land Company in that month. Meeting in Hartford in October, these fifty-three men elected seven directors: Henry Champion, Moses Cleaveland, Samuel W. Johnson, Ephraim Kirby, Samuel Mather, Jr., Roger Newberry and Oliver Phelps. The company determined to survey its property into townships five miles square, and Moses Cleaveland was appointed General Agent to supervise the work.

THE FIRST SURVEYING PARTY

Moses Cleaveland was a prominent and respected citizen of Canterbury, Connecticut. He had graduated from Yale University and was a practicing lawyer, Brigadier General of militia, and Representative in the Legislature. About forty years old at this time, he was described as "a short, thick-set man with a broad face, a dark complexion and coarse features. . . . able and shrewd in his negotiations with the Indians." In the winter of 1795-96 he gathered together the Reserve's first surveying party and made plans to bargain with the Indians for their claims to the Western Reserve.

To make the western trip, Cleaveland chose experienced men. Augustus Porter of Salisbury was the principal surveyor and deputy to Cleaveland. For seven years Porter had been surveying the area near Buffalo and was known to be a natural woodsman, a man familiar with frontier wilderness. From the journals of two of the other surveyors, we can read an almost complete account of the party's work. Seth Pease, astronomer and third in command, and John Milton Holley recorded for us an exciting version of their western adventures.

The party also included Joshua Stow who was in charge of provisions (the first building at Conneaut was named Stow's Castle in his honor). There was Theodore Shepard, physician, and Joseph Tinker, head boatman. Camp cook was James Hamilton who, in Holley's opinion, was sometimes "very cross and lazy." In addition, thirty-five others served as axemen, chainmen and rodmen. Among the latter was Charles Parker who was to become the first settler in what is now Lake County.

Six others joined the expedition making a total of fifty-two. Nathan Perry and Nathan Chapman traded with the Indians and supplied the party with fresh meat. Elijah Gun and his wife Anna took charge of the supplies at Conneaut. Job P. Stiles and his wife Tabitha Cumi looked after the company's stores in Cleveland when it was laid out as headquarters for the group.

THE SURVEYING TEAM SETS OUT

John Holley's journal begins, "This day, April 28, 1796, started for Lake Erie and lodged the third night at Wendells Hotel, Albany."

From there the group proceeded to Schenectady and up the Mohawk River. Part of them continued on to Canandaigua and Buffalo, driving "thirteen horses and some cattle." The rest, with five supply boats, crossed the portage to Oneida Lake and went down the Oswego River to Lake Ontario. Here they were held up for five weeks, first to obtain permission from the British to pass Fort Oswego, then because struck by a storm which destroyed one boat and damaged another.

On June 21 at Buffalo Moses Cleaveland met Iroquois representatives at a council fire to smoke the peace pipe and bargain for the Indians' hunting claims to the country which he was about to survey. For nearly a week Cleaveland entertained the Indians with feasting, drinking and dancing. Finally an agreement was made which cleared the way for white settlement as far west as the Cuyahoga River.

NEW CONNECTICUT

Moving westward through the wilderness, Cleaveland's group approached the boundary of their destination. At the end of the afternoon of July 4, Seth Pease found the cornerstone of Pennsylvania, the land party assembled and "gave three cheers precisely at 5 o'clock P. M." as they stepped onto the Western Reserve. An hour later they met the boats at Conneaut Creek, and all joined together to celebrate their arrival on the Fourth of July. "Tinker lined up the men and fired a Federal salute of 15 rounds, and then the 16th in honor of New Connecticut. We gave three cheers and christened the place Fort Independence." After several toasts had been proposed, the celebration was closed with another three cheers, and the party "supped and retired in remarkably good order."

A few days later the surveyors started work. From the cornerstone Pease had found, they traveled south on the Pennsylvania line, which had been surveyed ten years before but was now well overgrown. The going was rugged over rocks and ridges, through timber and swamp, and across streams and rivers. It took them just two weeks to trace the line sixty-eight miles south to the 41° parallel, and here they "set up a chestnut post, sixteen inches by twelve." The party divided into four groups to run range lines from this base line (the 41° parallel) back to the Lake. The north-south range lines were run perpendicular to the base line every five miles and numbered one, two, three, and so on from east to west. Later the township lines were run five miles apart parallel to the base line, and also were numbered one, two, three, etc., from south to north. Painesville, for example, before it was given a name, was known as Township No. 11, in Range No. 8.

FOUNDING THE CITY OF CLEVELAND

While Pease and his group were cutting range lines, Moses Cleaveland and a few others went by boat to lay out the city which the Connecticut Land Company had decided should be the center of the Reserve on the shores of Lake Erie. A short distance up the Cuyahoga where an Indian trail crossed the River, the party landed. Cleaveland climbed the bluff, paced out a generous ten acre public square and directed his men to plot a town around it. This public square is still the heart of a city which bears the name of its forthright founder.

CUTTING MORE LINES

Meanwhile, Augustus Porter, the principal surveyor, followed the shore line of Lake Erie to map its exact location. He started at the Pennsylvania corner and, although Cleaveland's agreement with the Indians had said that the white men would not cross the Cuyahoga River, he took the risk and ran his line the full one hundred and twenty miles due west to Sandusky Bay.

The other teams moved their lines slowly through the deep woods. The axemen had to clear a way through brush and brier, often chopping down large trees to make a path, so that the surveyors could see ahead to take compass sights and the chainmen could get through in a straight line to do the measuring. All the men tramped and slept without shelter. On many days the rains were so heavy they could not work, and under these conditions it is not hard to understand why they lost other days through illness. Time and again they ran out of food, often having to return to Cleveland or Conneaut for supplies. A few extracts from their journals describe their living conditions.

Holley wrote on Tuesday, July 12, 1796, that: "In the morning we breakfast in our camp by the little brook, and left the pack horse men to come on after us, but when we had proceeded about a mile, we sent back a hand to tell the men to go around the swamp with the horses, but the swamp continued, and we ran on until night. Here being a hemlock ridge, we were in hopes the horses would be able to find us, but alas! we were obliged to make a little camp of boughs, strike up a fire, and go to bed supperless. In the day time I had eat raspberries, gooseberries, wintergreen berries, and in the night I began to grow sick at my stomach . . . Mr. Pease too had a turn of the cramp, in consequence of travelling all day in the water. We all rose early in the morning, with meagre looks and somewhat faint for want of eating and drinking, for where we camped there was no water."

Holley continues on September 22: "Discovered a bear swimming across the river. Porter and myself jumped into a canoe and paddled after him, while another man went with a gun by the shore. But there was such a noise and hallooing, that the bear swam back and escaped. Munson caught a rattlesnake which was boiled and ate."

"The muskitos are the plentiest I ever found them and, like the furnace of the King of Babylon, heated with seven fold rage. I never was so tormented with them before. Their wrath increases as their time grows short. So greedy are they as to light on the Company's glass [the compass] and try to pierce it with their bills: I suppose deceived by the agitation of the needle and expecting blood instead of magnetism."

THE END OF THE FIRST SURVEYING TRIP

When the surveyors departed October 21, 1796, for their eastern homes, they left eleven people on the Reserve. The Stiles in Cleveland had Captain Edward Paine, Jr., as a boarder. He had come in the summer with his father from Aurora, New York, to trade with the Indians. It was undoubtedly through young Paine's efforts that the Stiles were supplied with fresh meat through the winter.

Food was not so plentiful for the residents of Conneaut. The Guns had as neighbors the first independent settlers in the Reserve, James and Eunice Kingsbury, their thirteen year old nephew, and three children, aged one, two and three. Another baby was born to them in the depth of winter. Their supplies were used up, and the mother was too sick and weak to nurse the baby. Kingsbury dragged a sled to the settlement at Erie to get a bushel of wheat to keep his family alive, but the baby died of starvation. When Pease returned the following May, he wrote: "Mr. Kingsbury, his wife and one child, were in a low state of health, to whom we administered what relief we could." Both families had had enough of Conneaut, and soon moved to Cleveland.

The directors of the Connecticut Land Company had been overly optimistic when they believed the region could be mapped in one summer. They were also disappointed to learn the total acreage in the Western Reserve was far less than the original estimate. Augustus Porter, when he extended his survey of the shore to Sandusky Bay, found that Lake Erie drops southwest much more sharply than early maps had shown. Instead of having a territory over 3,000,000 acres, the Land Company discovered there were actually less than 2,500,000 acres of solid ground. The rest lay under the waters of Lake Erie. This was to be a severe financial loss to the Company, which was also faced with further surveying.

THE SURVEY IS COMPLETED

The second summer, 1797, the men sent out by the Connecticut Land Company were led by Seth Hart, superintendent, and Seth Pease, principal surveyor. With the experience of the previous year to his advantage, Pease had a well-organized group with eight surveyors instead of four as the year before. Spafford, Stoddard and Warren returned, Atwater, Landon, and Shepard were promoted from chainmen, and two new men were hired. Their fifty-two assistants included five of the former group.

Pease had also learned something about the problem of supplies and came well-prepared. He itemized the equipment sent off with each gang: "Pork, flour, tea, chocolate, sugar, ginger, spirits, vinegar, cheese, pepper, empty bags [for baking bread in front of the camp fire], candles, fire steel and punk, a tent, axes and hatchets, pocket compass, measuring pins, salt, soap, a camp kettle, one frying pan, needles and thread, and horses."

The success of the second summer was a credit to Pease's management, for the party was pursued by bad luck. On their way into the Reserve, David Eldridge drowned attempting to swim his horse across the Grand River. Later three other men drowned. Everyone suffered from fever and dysentery. The physician could give them little help, and three more men died. But, somehow, the little band struggled on, and at the end of the summer all township lines east of the Cuyahoga River were finished, Cleveland was laid out in lots of various sizes, and four townships had been surveyed into one hundred and sixty acre tracts.

THE LAND IS APPORTIONED

In the meantime, the Connecticut Land Company drafted a plan for apportioning its holdings. Of all the townships surveyed, six of the best were set aside to be offered for sale to actual settlers. The proceeds of these sales were used by the Company to pay the cost of the surveying and the land agents who conducted the sales. Of these six best townships, three were chosen from our present Lake County: Madison, Mentor and Willoughby.

The next four best townships were each surveyed into one hundred tracts to be distributed by lot among the shareholders. In these four was Perry.

Of the remaining townships, eight were chosen as "standard," that is, of average quality of soil, ease of cultivation, and water supply. There were also twenty-four whole or partial townships (those where the Lake cut into the five mile square) which was set aside to be divided into "equalizing" portions to bring the inferior townships up to the value of the eight "standard" ones. These "equalizing" parcels included Concord,

Kirtland, Painesville (a partial township), Madison Gore and Willoughby Gore (the pieces over and above the five mile square).

This arrangement for the division of the land followed the pattern used by the early colonists as they purchased more land from the Indians. It was an honest effort to see that each investor received his fair share of the Company's holdings and seems to have worked to everyone's satisfaction. Its details are of interest to us because they show how highly the surveyors valued our Lake County land.

THE IMPORTANCE OF THE SURVEY

Today land records are commonplace to us. Cities, villages and farms are all mapped, described and recorded at county courthouses. There is seldom any difficulty in obtaining an abstract to show that boundaries are accurately drawn, that title is clear through each past owner and is unencumbered by old mortgages. Behind this simple transaction is the toil of the first surveyors. Their enterprise, endurance, and their skill form one of the real sagas of American life. The first surveyors on the Western Reserve were typical of the men who, though they receive little recognition, make our investment in a business or our purchase of a home, easy and orderly.

After the surveyors came the pioneer settlers. They were to build in the virgin forests along Lake Erie's southern shore the homes they so earnestly desired. Between the years 1797 and 1817, one by one the wilderness townships of our present Lake County welcomed their first permanent settlers.

Chapter III

Our Stout Hearted Pioneers

In the spring of 1797 Charles Parker returned with the surveying party for another season as axeman and chainman. The hardships of the first summer had not lessened his enthusiasm for the Reserve. Rich fertile soil and gently rolling country promised him a better future than the rock covered hills of his native Vermont. He came to make his home here and brought his wife and their meagre household furnishings. During the summer he interrupted his work with the surveying party to clear a little space in the heavy forest at a place, described by one of the surveyors, "about 19 miles by the lake shore from the Cuyahoga, [where] a creek comes in, which forms a large marsh lying a mile along shore and on an average 100 rods wide." Still known to us today as Mentor Marsh, this was the home of the first white family in what we know as Lake County.

MENTOR MARSH SETTLEMENT

Surrounded on three sides by dense woods full of bear, wolves, rattlesnakes and howling wildcats as well as more friendly game, the little clearing opened on the vast unpredictable Lake. Mrs. Parker had to be a stalwart woman to face the loneliness of this bewildering new world when her husband left her to finish his job with the surveying crew. She must have gladly welcomed any of the surveying party who passed by. They were undoubtedly happy to stop for a rest and a woman's cooking at her crude log cabin, the only home between Cleveland and Conneaut.

Before the summer was over, a second clearing was made at Mentor Marsh by Ebenezer Merry and two other young men who came from Avon, New York. Walking to Buffalo, they procured a small open boat to carry them and their provisions. They followed the shore line, rowing by day and camping at night on land. Near the Parkers they built a rough bark shanty and began the arduous task of clearing a field for crops.

Merry and his friends piled brush high to dry before burning. They chopped down small trees to cut for firewood. From the larger trees they stripped a circle of bark, a method called "girdling," used by the early pioneers to kill a tree. In this way the next spring no leaves came to shade crops planted under the girdled trees and between the smaller stumps. Eventually the dead trees were cut down for lumber and the uprooted stumps turned into a rough fence.

All this work was done with an axe and a crude plow. These early settlers could bring only the most essential equipment in their small boat. However, they worked hard and at the end of the summer of 1797 both Charles Parker and Ebenezer Merry had cleared enough land to plant a crop of winter wheat.

MERRY AND HIS SHOES

During the summer Merry lost his shoes. Having no shoe blacking to shine them, one evening he had covered them with a coating of grease mixed with burnt straw and set them outside his door to dry. In the morning they were gone. Supposing that one of his companions had hidden them as a joke, he made no comment and went off to his chopping barefooted. Soon he found one and then the other shoe. Wolves had taken them and so mutilated them licking off the grease that they were no longer fit to wear. Years later Merry claimed that his feet were so tough by fall that he could stamp chestnuts from their burrs!

Still barefoot, according to the story, Merry returned to Avon in the late fall. The other young men went home also, leaving the Parkers alone for the winter, their only neighbors five families in Cleveland and ten in Youngstown. The next spring Merry returned with his brother Hosmer, and two other couples joined the settlement: Mr. and Mrs. Jared Ward and Mr. and Mrs. Moses Parks. Moses Parks had been a Baptist minister before he decided to try his luck pioneering. To him belongs the story of the first marriage in what later became Lake County.

THE FIRST MARRIAGE

John Hamilton, a handsome young man, lived in Newburgh, now the south eastern section of Cleveland. Not content with bachelor life in the wilderness and hearing that there was a pretty young widow in Harpersfield, he saddled his horse and set out to look her over. Apparently he liked what he saw for he soon persuaded Mrs. Mingus to return with him. They started off on horseback with the widow's child on his lap and Mrs. Mingus behind him riding on her feather bed for a saddle. At Marsh Settlement they met with an unexpected difficulty. Mr. Parks refused to marry them on the grounds that he had abandoned the ministry. His resolve soon melted under the persuasion of the young lady and he yielded to her pleading. He performed the ceremony, and, so the tale goes, the couple continued on their journey to Newburgh to live happily ever after.

NEIGHBORING SETTLEMENTS BEGIN

Two of our natural harbors were doorways to two neighboring settlements. One, at Harpersfield, while in today's Ashtabula County, is still part of our Lake County history. Alexander Harper came from New York State and had been a Colonel in the Revolutionary Army. With his family and friends, a group of twenty-three in all, he had chartered the only sailing vessel on Lake Erie to carry them and their goods west from Buffalo. The party landed on June 28, 1798, at the mouth of a creek (now the end of Dock Road in Madison Township). The following day the group started south, soon finding the township line tramped out by the surveyors two years before. At what is now the South Ridge, an Indian trail crossed the surveyor's track and the Harpers turned east to settle just beyond the border of present day Lake County. The junction of the two forest paths became the crossroads at Unionville.

Colonel Harper died at the end of the summer and was buried on the southeast corner of the crossroads. His is the oldest marked grave in the Western Reserve.

The other neighboring settlement was opened by Turhand Kirtland, land agent of the Connecticut Land Company and a large land holder in our township named for him. On June 3, 1798, he arrived at the mouth of the Grand River with Law, Beard, Tomlinson, Pond and the Umberfields with five children. According to Kirtland's diary, they went up the river about four miles "to the Indian Town at the old fording place, found several houses and a large settlement [of Indians]." Leaving the Umberfields with the supplies, the men blazed a trail to Burton with two yokes of oxen and some provisions on a sled. They reached their destination on June 15. This Burton trail was to become an important frontier artery.

DAVID ABBOTT AND THE FIRST MILL

In this year 1798 the first settler came to what is now Willoughby. David Abbott, born in Brookfield, Massachusetts, had studied law at Yale and like many of our other pioneers moved to New York State. He started his practice in Rome. Hearing stories of greater profits, he abandoned law and spent the summer of 1797 trading with the Indians as far west as Detroit. He had visited a few of them at Charlton (or Carlton), the old French trading post at the mouth of the Chagrin River. He liked the place and on his return trip explored it more fully. During the winter he went to Connecticut to purchase the land he had picked out. He found that to encourage settlement in this township, the Land Company was offering $200 or a loan of $500 at 6% interest to the man who would build the first grist mill. Abbott seized the opportunity.

He returned home and made arrangements for his move to the Reserve. Leaving his wife and year old son with her parents in Rome, he hired several men, and they started out in February with a yoke of oxen, one cow and a sled loaded with their tools and provisions. When they reached Lake Erie they traveled over the ice close to shore, and they arrived at the Chagrin River March 22, 1798. The men first built a cabin and then planted some corn, potatoes and "garden sass" in the old trading post clearing. Next they started on the mill. Among the men who helped Abbott were Ebenezer Merry from Marsh Settlement, Peter French who came with Abbott from New York State and Ebenezer Smith, a blacksmith. Smith made the tools to cut the mill stones from boulders found in the area. Completed in the fall, this was the first mill to operate in the Western Reserve, and a welcome addition it must have been to the pioneers. The name of Charlton was soon changed by popular usage to Chagrin Mills, and then shortened to Chagrin.

WALWORTH AND PAINE — PAINESVILLE

The winter of 1798-99 was a far more sociable one for the Parker family than had been the one before. They had neighbors close at hand, friends in Chagrin Mills, Burton and Harpersfield, and Cleveland's population had risen to nine households. Added to these, Marsh Settlement had a most interesting boarder, John Walworth. Born in Connecticut, well-educated for his time, he had spent several years at sea. This winter he was returning from an extensive trip in the unexplored west and his stories must have enlivened many a long evening for the little community. He had come to investigate this area at the suggestion of his friend and neighbor, General Edward Paine. Walworth took time to explore thoroughly before returning to his home in Aurora, New York. He then made a brief trip to Connecticut to purchase two thousand acres lying east of the Grand River on the lake shore.

In the fall of 1799 Walworth came out to his land with his hired man John Miller, two horses, a yoke of oxen and a cow. From Buffalo they drove the cattle along the beach. The Lake was unusually low during these early years of settlement, and it was generally easy to ford streams by driving the animals out into the shallow water to the sand bars, which still run along our shoreline.

Arriving at their destination, the men cleared a site about two miles up the river and raised a large double cabin. They split long "shakes" from oak logs to shingle it. Leaving Miller to fasten these in place, Walworth returned east for the two families. On February 20, 1800, he started west again with two sleighs, each drawn by a team of horses. One held his wife, four children, a young cousin and a colored girl. The other, driven by a hired man, brought Mrs. Miller and her two children. Arriving at Buffalo, Walworth rented a house for the women, and the two men went back to bring on two sleds full of their household goods and farm tools.

From Buffalo to Erie the families made good time over the frozen lake, but when the men were returning with their second load, spring thaws had set in. One of the teams broke through the ice and Walworth had to go back to Schenectady to replace the lost farm equipment. He returned to Erie by wagon and there his party embarked in open boats for Grand River, finally arriving at their new home at the end of April.

A few weeks later, the Walworths were joined by their Aurora neighbor, General Edward Paine. Paine and his son had returned home from their trading venture of 1796-97 enthusiastic about the Reserve lands. General Paine went to Connecticut in 1798, bought one thousand acres, returned to New York State and organized a group of sixty-six settlers. His home was next to Walworth's, between Grand River and the Lake, and the other families settled near by.

Early in 1801 Walworth went east after goods and provisions. He brought back Mrs. David Abbott and her son to join Abbott at Chagrin. Abraham Tappen, the first school teacher of the settlement, also came with Walworth and boarded with him four or five years.

LIFE AMONG THE PIONEERS

The first Fourth of July celebration in the area was held at Walworth's home, "Blooming Grove," soon after he returned. An old account of the party reads: "About ten o'clock, the people who had already assembled under the bower in front of the cabin, were agreeably surprised by the approaching and soul-stirring sound of martial music. Such an occurance to them was unexpected. The mystery was soon explained. Several families from Marsh Settlement had planned to meet first at ['Elysian Fields'], General Paine's home, and they, together with the General's family, were to go up the river to Walworth's in a boat. Joel Paine agreed to blow the fife. Someone volunteered to beat the drum, and the boat was rowed and polled up the river, the music in full strain. On arriving at the landing, the company marched up the hill, two abreast, General Paine and Dr. Bond at the head; and were received by those already assembled, in open ranks. An orator was called upon and delivered an extemporary oration, replete with sound political maxims, with a commendable sprinkling of patriotism. The table was spread and the dinner served under the bowery. After the removal of the cloth, toasts were offered and drank with much glee, sixteen in number, at the time the number of the states."

Another party long remembered was given the following year by Mrs. Alexander Harper for her daughters. Friends were invited from Burton, Painesville, Windsor and Austinburg. The rare dainty offered for the occasion was wheat cakes fried in bear grease. Mrs. Harper, a good singer, performed for the company and the young people danced to her music. Not long after the party, her son John married one of the guests. In 1802 Mr. and Mrs. John Harper set up housekeeping on the west side of the Unionville crossroads and were the first settlers in Chapin, eventually known as Madison Township.

SETTLEMENTS IN OTHER TOWNSHIPS

The year 1802 also marked the first settlement in Concord Township. Thomas Jordan from Mifflin County, Pennsylvania, cleared land and built a home on the trail Turhand Kirtland and his friends had cut to Burton. The following year he sent for his wife and eight children, and they came with their household goods on three pack horses, making the journey in three weeks. The Jordans were the first family from Pennsylvania to come to our territory. Most Pennsylvania pioneers settled in the southern part of the Reserve, not often coming as far north as this to find their homesites.

Settlements in Leroy Township (named first "Chesterfield" by the Connecticut Land Company) were made in 1802 and 1803. Colonel Amasa Clapp of Massachusetts, a Connecticut Land Company shareholder, had drawn lots in township No. 10, range No. 7, and in 1802 he sent his sons Paul and Elah to open up his land. The young men built a cabin, cleared six acres and sowed it in wheat, which next year yielded fifteen to twenty bushels an acre.

SPENCER PHELPS' ACCOUNT

Leroy Township's other pioneer, Spencer Phelps, left us his account, written fifty years later, of his trip to the Western Reserve: "At the age of twenty-one in 1803 I left home in Massachusetts on horseback with a neighbor of mine for Ohio. . . . There was no bridge west of Buffalo. The first house was at Cataragus [sic], where there was a ferry. . . . The road was almost impassable, sometimes we had to go onto the beach and around the rocks where the water was up to the horse's sides for some distance. . . . At Erie there were about 20 houses. From there I came in an open boat with Edward and Asabel Paine.

"On the first day of June, after 21 days of hard travel, I reached General Paine's where there was a home for all who came. After staying a day or two I found where I could get provisions." Phelps worked to pay for his supplies, then went on to Leroy to begin clearing his land.

He continues: "The year before two men by the name of Clapp had been there . . . and built a house. Jonathan Russell took up a lot so there were four of us (all males) in a family. We planted some potatoes that grew well. Toward fall our provisions ran out. We had no bread and could not get any. We soon devoured our potatoes and had nothing left. The wheat was good when harvested. We pounded out some and boiled it to eat with milk, but it would not soften, it was a hard job to eat and we soon gave it up. . . . We held a council and agreed to pound out some wheat and go to mill, but the trouble was where to go. . . . We built a sled, split out some boards for a bottom, loaded up and I started for Humphrey's mill in Austinburg with a yoke of oxen. I had to go through Thompson, Trumbull and Austinburg. There was one house on the road, but it was empty. I followed the Old Girdled Road . . . It was the first team that ever went through. Sometimes I was in the road, then on one side, then on the other. However, I cut my way and got through the second day after dark. I got my grinding done that night and started back the next day, but had to lay in the woods that night. When I returned there was great rejoicing."

VILLAGES IN PAINESVILLE TOWNSHIP

Pioneer population increased and the first villages began to appear on the Reserve. The next few years saw three towns growing in Painesville Township. In 1803 Joseph Rider built the first permanent cabin at the mouth of the Grand River, and the same year Abraham Skinner and Eleazer Paine laid out the town of New Market farther up the river. They built cabins for their families and a warehouse to store the goods they expected to arrive at their landing place. New Market, though it was to enjoy prominence as county seat for a few years, did not grow as its founders hoped and before long was just another pasture.

In 1805 Skinner was employed by Henry Champion, of the Connecticut Land Company to lay out another town two miles south at a thin spot in the forest, where sandy soil and scrub oak growth led the settlers to name the area "Oak Openings." The new town was called "Champion."

A great dream in those days was to found a town and have it named after you. Beyond giving a public square "to be used as a park forever," there is no record that Champion did much to develop his town, but it did prosper. Its location at the junction of the Lake Road, the Burton Road, the Austinburg and Chagrin Roads was a leading factor in its success. Later the town's name was changed to Painesville to conform with that of the township which had been named to honor General Paine's early interest in the area.

SAMUEL HUNTINGTON COMES TO PAINESVILLE

Samuel Huntington wrote to Moses Cleaveland in 1801: "I have moved my Patriarchal Caravan through the wilderness to this Canaan. I was nine days on the Journey, with two Waggons [sic], ten oxen, three horses, seven Cows, and eighteen persons in my Retinue. We slept seven nights in the open air, and pursued the same rout [sic] that my former Waggons [sic] went, but our road wanted cutting again, on account of fresh Windfalls; our Women and Children supported the Journey with courage and spirit." Bringing much more equipment than most pioneers, Huntington's party had traveled from Norwich, Connecticut, across Pennsylvania to Warren and north to Cleveland.

A member of a prominent New England family, Samuel Huntington had graduated from Yale, been admitted to the bar, and traveled in Europe before he came to the Reserve. After a few years in Cleveland he found the climate unsatisfactory and began looking for another home. At this time John Walworth was appointed Collector of the Port and Postmaster of Cleveland. The two men solved their housing problems by exchanging property, and the Huntingtons moved to Painesville in 1807.

On his arrival in the Reserve Huntington had immediately become active in local politics. He was one of our delegates to Ohio's Constitutional Convention and was elected senator to Ohio's first Legislature, serving as its president. At the same time he was one of the three judges of Ohio's Supreme Court and also Supervisor of Highways. In 1808 he became our state's second elected governor.

Interested in his new community, as well as the affairs of Ohio, Huntington with Abraham Skinner laid out the town of Grandon (now Fairport Harbor) to provide this area with a port. He was a man of small stature but had abounding energy. A natural leader, he was popular and his business methods were efficient and honest. His personality added vitality and enterprise to our community. He died in 1817 from injuries received while supervising repairs on the road from his home to the harbor.

PERRY TOWNSHIP IS SETTLED

The pioneer of Perry Township was Ezra Beebe who opened up a clearing on the South Ridge in 1808. It was still wild and lonely country. Spencer Phelps, across the Grand River, wrote, "We had trouble with our neighbors sometimes, for if we got any hogs, [neighbor] bear would eat them, and if we had any sheep [neighbor] wolf would kill them, and [neighbor] fox took our hens. But I had some satisfaction for I have killed nine bears, besides elk, deer, turkeys, and coons." Slowly the stream of immigration flowed into our townships and orderly communities grew in the forests.

CENTERVILLE

About this time a village, known for many years as Centerville, was gathering in Chapin Township. Jesse Ladd wrote to his wife in Berkshire County, Massachusetts: "I have been very busy exploring and viewing the country since my arrival here and must say with perfect truth and satisfaction that the country appears much better to me than it did last summer. The land I have bought is as good as any in the country; the lot adjoining is settled with three or four families of very agreeable and respectable people from Willington, Connecticut, and instead of a howling wilderness adjoining the place where I intend to live, there is now an opening of from thirty to forty acres, and fifteen acres of as good corn as ever I saw in my life. Crops generally in this country are very good. Wheat is excellent and grass is good . . . I shall be happy to cultivate next summer."

KIRTLAND TOWNSHIP

In May of 1811 Christopher Crary arrived in Unionville after a thirty-two day trip by ox team from Berkshire County, Massachusetts. He left his family with Deacon Martin, an old neighbor, while he selected land. He picked out a tract in the southern part of Kirtland Township and moved his family to Mentor to stay with Judge Clapp while he built his cabin seven miles away at what became known as Peck's Corners.

Later Crary's son, Christopher Gore Crary, wrote a description of the county about the time of his family's arrival. "Madison, I think, was more thickly populated at that time than any other township in the county, and Unionville was as large as Painesville." Names he recollected were the Nathan Warners, Judge Tappen, Potter, the Cunninghams, Ladd, Brewster, Turner, Wheeler and Mixer. "Perry was then an almost unbroken wilderness." In Painesville he listed General Paine, General King, Eli Bond, Uri Seeley, Sessions, Skinner, Hall, Samuel Butler, Williams, Frank Paine, Mr. Pepoon and sons. In Concord there was Benai Jones, Nye and Blish. Mentor had Truman Griswold, who "did so much to rid the section of wolves," Fobes, Judge Clapp, Warren Corning, a Mr. Bacon, Abel and Jonathan Russell. At Chagrin were Christopher Colson, Lewis Abbott, Humphrey, the Wirts, Noel Worden, Holly Tanner, and up the river a Mr. Judd, Lowell Eames and Mr. Freer. In Kirtland Crary remembered one family in the township, John Moore, who soon left. Peter French moved over from Mentor, and John Parris, Isaac Morley and Titus Billings came soon after.

THE WAR OF 1812

Young Crary also left a description of the effect of the War of 1812 on the settlements of the Reserve. He wrote: "The War of 1812 put a stop to all further immigration to the Reserve, and some who were here left. It was a time of great alarm, especially after the surrender of Detroit by Hull. There seemed nothing to prevent the British and Indians from coming down the lake, both by land and by water, pillaging, marauding and destroying everything on the southern shore. There was a call for all capable of bearing arms to congregate at Sundusky in order to take a stand against the expected invaders." A number started from this area "and went as far as Sandusky. In the meantime General [William Henry] Harrison had pushed forward . . . and by good generalship succeeded in repulsing and scattering the Indians. . . . They became discouraged, deserted; the British retired to safer quarters. There being no further danger in that quarter our volunteers returned. . . . Our next great scare was at the time of Perry's victory. We distinctly heard the cannonading. The sound seemed to be to the right of Cleveland and a little further off, and we thought it must be a naval battle. . . . It was several days before our fears were allayed by news of the result."

Perry's famous message, "We have met the enemy and they are ours," reached our settlements in the middle of September 1813, and with it the war moved from the Reserve. But fighting went on in other parts of the country until 1815. With peace came many settlers, and in 1817 the last of our early communities was founded.

WICKLIFFE, CHAGRIN TOWNSHIP

In that year of 1817 William Jones came from Haddam, Connecticut, with his wife, daughter and son-in-law, a man by the name of Tarbell. They had traveled in two covered wagons drawn by three oxen and one cow, making the journey in six weeks. First they went into Cleveland, but finding the soil too sandy for farming, they retraced their steps for fifteen miles to what became Wickliffe. On a knoll they built a double log cabin, which they were able to replace in three years with a clapboard house.

In the twenty years since the first settlers arrived in what is now our Lake County, living conditions had improved and transportation had become easier, but it was still a long way to markets. Men recognized the need for better roads and harbors to take produce to customers and bring back merchandise to the farmers. Our stout-hearted pioneers realized they had more to do than build cabins and clear fields in order to make a prosperous community. They faced the never-ending struggle for enlarged and improved means of transportation.

Chapter IV

Lifelines to Progress

Our pioneers were more fortunate than many frontiersmen because they found a primitive transportation system literally built into the land. Not only was there the lake for water travel, but there were also natural sand ridges parallel to the shoreline, ideal for early trails and already well marked by the Indians. These ridges, left from lakes formed by the retreating glacier, were indeed our first roads and they remained important as lifelines of communication and commerce from the earliest days to the Twentieth Century.

THE GIRDLED ROAD

In the summer of 1797, surveyors Seth Pease, Moses Warren and Theodore Shepard had recommended a route for a road from the Pennsylvania line to the Cuyahoga River. It would pass through present-day Conneaut, Kingsville, Sheffield and Plymouth Townships, cross the Grand River at the Indian ford in Austinburg, continue through Harpersfield, Thompson, Leroy, Concord and Kirtland Townships. From the Chagrin River to Cleveland the route followed the Indian's middle ridge trail.

Connecticut Land Company directors realized the importance of such a road for promoting land sales and as a means of communication between settlements. The following spring they signed a $6,000 contract with General Simon Perkins "that a road be cut to the width of twenty-five feet, and that the large trees be girded [sic] to a width of thirty-three feet, and that bridges be built over streams too deep to ford." Perkins' construction camp was in what became Concord Township near where the path to Burton would cross the new road.

Descriptions of traveling this road were left by early settlers. Of her wedding journey to Mentor, Mrs. Ebenezer Merry wrote (in the third person): "On the 14th day of May, 1800, he and his wife started for Ohio on horseback accompanied by a younger brother. . . . they traveled west. . . . until they came to the east boundary of what was called New Connecticut, from which they traveled by a road newly cut by the Connecticut Land Company.

"The balance of their journey they forded creeks and rivers, sometimes in canoes, swimming their horses. At a branch of the Ashtabula they crossed upon a tree which was part of the way under water, so they were obliged to wade in the water quite deep upon the log, holding onto the limbs to steady themselves . . ."

Another traveler, Missionary Badger, bluntly referred to it in his journal in 1802 as "this miserable road." Spencer Phelps' description of his trip on the road in 1803 gives no sign of improvement. Before long, traffic moved to the sand ridges, and all that is left today of the Girdled Road is the section in Leroy and Concord Townships.

THE SETTLERS MAKE ROADS

Visiting friends, getting to the mills at Chagrin and Austinburg, attending court sessions or paying taxes at Warren and later at Chardon were all reasons for forging more roads. The Harpers improved on the surveyor's path from the lake to Unionville. Another route opened by pioneers from New Market to Burton was further cleared, widened and extended to Warren. The Paines and Walworths, with the Harpers and Austins, cut a road along the Indian trail that is now Route 84 to connect their settlements. By 1802 the Indian path from Grand River to Abbott's mill was a wagon trace, eventually becoming Mentor Avenue. Soon after Ohio became a state, several roads were built radiating from the capital, and our Chillicothe Road was one of these.

There is preserved an interesting contract made by Andrew Cowee in October 1804, to build eight and a quarter miles of the New Market-Warren road, starting from the Grand River, the work to be done by the following May.

"All timber and brush shall be cut and cleared off ten feet each way from the center of said road making it 20 feet in width. The bushes to be cut close to the ground leaving the stumps of all timbers not more than one foot in height. Places naturally inclined to be wet and mirey shall be made passable by a causeway sixteen foot wide to be made of timber covered with earth. Small streams that are difficult to pass shall be bridged. When the road passes on sidling ground it shall be dug horizontally into the hill so that the way is solid ground. In ascending, hills shall not have a greater elevation from a horizontal line than 15 degrees."

CORDUROY ROADS

Causeways were made by laying trees crosswise, corduroy fashion, and were not often covered with earth. There was no road machinery to dig, haul or level. Men paid their taxes by furnishing their own labor and their teams for road work. They shoveled by hand and loaded the soil into their wagons or sleds. When a road was passable, the farmers were much too anxious to get back to their crops to think about a rider's comfort. Then time, weather and use might blot out their efforts.

Forty years after Cowee signed his contract, the famous English author Charles Dickens, describing a trip on such an Ohio road, wrote, "At one time we were all flung together in a heap at the bottom of the coach, and at another time we were crushing our heads against the roof. The slightest of the jolts with which the ponderous carriage fell from log to log, was enough, it seemed, to have dislocated every bone in the body."

The name of Corduroy Road in Mentor is a reminder of the early days before men had time, skill or equipment to dig drainage ditches, haul gravel and properly care for a road. Even into the present century Black Brook was an unconquered marsh where men depended on the old corduroy method to bridge the muck. A pause at the edge of the road today will indicate what Cowee meant by "places naturally inclined to be wet and mirey."

BRIDGES

The early Indian trails crossed the rivers where the water spread out over shale bottom, often just above a little falls, where water was clear and footing solid. Our pioneers soon learned to use the same fording places. Joel Scott built the first bridge across Grand River in 1806, connecting New Market with the Paines' and Huntingtons' homes. However, this bridge crossed a deep part of the river where the current was strong, and it was washed out in a few years by spring floods. A second bridge was built in 1810 at a better fording spot a little below the foot of what is now Main Street, Painesville.

In 1818 William Darby made a trip from New York to Detroit. He described Painesville and its new bridge: "Upon the left bank of the Grand River stands the flourishing village of Painesville, the richest and most commercial in the county, containing a number of stores, taverns, mills, and other machinery; a post office and a fine wooden bridge over the Grand River."

Covered bridges, first built in Philadelphia in 1805, soon became popular here. The barn-like construction was strong and could be put together comparatively easily by the early engineers. The roof and siding protected the bridge's supporting timbers from weathering. Covered bridges were sturdy affairs and had a long life. The last one in Lake County, on Blair Road in Perry Township, was torn down in 1952, but there are still many left in Ashtabula County.

MAIL ROUTES

Communication between the scattered settlements gradually grew easier as the roads and bridges were built. In 1803 mail service was begun from Warren north to Austinburg, west to Unionville, Painesville and on to Cleveland, returning the same way. A man named McIlvain made the one hundred and eighty mile round trip on foot every week, carrying the mail in his high beaver hat. When the route was extended to Detroit, he made the trip on horseback. In 1811 service was begun between Buffalo and Cleveland, and Asher Bigelow made the round trip in twelve days. He collected postage, 25c paid on delivery, then equal in value to four pounds of butter or four dozen eggs.

The next improvement in mail service came with the advent of stage coaches. In the Cleveland *Gazette* August 11, 1818, the following advertisement appeared: "A mail stage has commenced running between this village and Painesville. It leaves Painesville at every Thursday at 4 o'clock p. m. and arrives at this place every Friday at 10 o'clock a. m. It leaves this village the same day at 2 o'clock p. m. and arrives in Painesville every Saturday at 8 o'clock a. m. Persons traveling to Painesville will find it to their interest to go in the stage as traveling can be done with greater facility than by riding a single horse and the expense is not so great."

Before long the trip was extended to Ashtabula, and in 1820 to Erie. Children of those days ran to the roadside to see the big coach, the prancing horses (four were used by 1820), and the driver, sitting high up, using his whip with a flourish. The horses were changed every ten or fifteen miles, and the driver blew his long horn as he approached the change point.

INNS AND TAVERNS

The mail and passenger coach line meant good business for the wayside inns. Besides stabling and feeding the horses, innkeepers provided passengers with rest and refreshment. The tap rooms were the village post offices, and the arrival of the stage was a good excuse to inquire for a letter, visit with one's friends, or hear world news from the travelers. Mingling with the crowd were roughly dressed immigrants, their teams of oxen standing in the innyard. Dining rooms were filled, bedrooms crowded, and many a man, rolled in his blankets, slept on the floor before the huge fireplace in the public room. Larger inns had a ballroom on the second floor, and evenings were occasionally enlivened by the young people of the neighborhood in their simple finery dancing to the tunes of the village fiddler.

Two of these old stage stops still serving travelers are Unionville Inn and Lutz's Inn at Painesville. In 1805 Ira Blanchard built a log cabin at the Unionville crossroads to accommodate travelers. The present building, constructed in 1818, was at the junction of the main Cleveland-Buffalo route and the road from Harper's Landing to Warren. Unionville Inn served two lines of stage coaches for many years. Business fell off when the railroad came, but except for a brief period of nine years, the Inn has continued to welcome visitors since it was opened.

Joseph Rider built a log cabin at Painesville in 1810, replaced it with a frame building in 1818, enlarged it in 1822. He cut a new road (now Walnut Street) at his own expense to bring the South Ridge traffic to his door — and to divert it from his rivals. At the river he boldly posted a sign: "One mile to the only tavern." There was still enough business for Captain Eaton at the corner of Johnny Cake Ridge and Chardon Road, for Hezikiah King's tavern and the Franklin House in the center of the village. After 1840 when his father died, Zerah Rider continued operating his inn until stage coach days were over. Rider Tavern was used for many years as the family home. Eventually the automobile brought business back to our roadside restaurants and the Inn was reopened to serve the public once again.

Many other inns flourished in our communities during the period from 1815 to 1860. Some have disappeared but a few still stand as large and comfortable homes, such as Jesse Ladd's tavern on the South Ridge in Madison Township. Lloyd's Tavern in Wickliffe, one of the most famous of the inns, is no longer standing. Built of brick made on the grounds, it was finished inside with handcarved woodwork. Lloyd's, the first stop out of Cleveland for change of horses, was very prosperous during stage coach days. Later, like Rider's, it served as the family home. The building was razed in 1949 to make way for the stores opposite the Junior High School.

THE TALE OF THE RUNAWAY STAGECOACH

An old issue of the Painesville *Republican* tells a story of a runaway stagecoach. "It seems that in stage coach days there was a driver named Frank Bryant, known then and later to every resident of this section. Bryant, so the story goes, was on his way to Cleveland with the coach, having as passengers a middle-aged lady and her charming daughter. At the Rider Tavern a stop was made while Bryant went inside to exchange greetings with the landlord and get a little something to take the 'wire edge off his whistle.' The horses became frightened and started to run, taking with them the coach and passengers.

"Sometime later when Bryant appeared at the doorway, wiping his mouth with the back of his hand, he was much surprised to find his rig gone. Running to the barn he threw a saddle on a horse and started at a fast clip towards the west. It was a long chase and a hot one, the coach horses running at top speed. Several times Bryant sighted the coach but it was not until Willoughby was reached that he caught up with it.

"At the doorway of the Willoughby Tavern the coach horses stopped as neatly as though the driver had been in the box, and Bryant was just in time to jump off his horse and open the coach door for his passengers. When the lady alighted Bryant expected she would be either frightened or mad, but instead she smiled and shook his hand, remarking, 'You are the first real driver we've had since we left Buffalo.' "

The tavern at which the horses stopped may have been Daniel Christy's, a building (torn down in 1962) at the northwest end of today's Pelton Street bridge. This bridge is at the pioneer crossing of the Chagrin River, once by ford, and then spanned by covered bridge. Farther up the hill there was the colorful Zebra Stage Coach House at the northwest corner of what is now Erie Street and the Nickle Plate Railroad crossing. Here the clapboards were painted alternately light green, yellow and white, and two porches, one above and one below, ran across the front of the building. The "Zebra" continued in use until destroyed by fire in 1879.

GRAND RIVER CARGOES

Although roads were being improved, it was still slow and expensive work to haul goods to market. Water transportation was used whenever possible. Commenting on this on a visit to Ohio in 1803, Thaddeus Mason Harris wrote: "Warren is a pleasant and thriving town, situated on Big Beaver Creek. . . . This creek opens up a communication by boats with Le Grand Riviere [sic], which flows into Lake Erie, obstructed by a short portage. Through this route is carried on a considerable trade, which is constantly increasing."

While we have no record of traffic with Warren, there is ample evidence of a Grand River navy plying between Painesville and Windsor in the southeast corner of Ashtabula County. The *Gregory*, a flat-bottomed boat thirty-five feet in length and five and a half feet wide, was used in a regular shipping business out of Harpersfield beginning in March, 1800, and was soon joined by other craft. The river was used, too, for logging. The squared timbers for Captain Skinner's warehouse at New Market were floated down stream from the sawmill at Austinburg.

HARBOR DEVELOPMENT

Darby's 1818 journal also described Fairport and its growing harbor. "Grand River is a stream of some consequence. . . . It is about seventy yards wide at the mouth, with seven foot water on the bar near the entrance into the Lake. The east bank rises to the height of 30 or 40 feet affording a very handsome site for a village. The harbor is excellent for such vessels whose whole draft of water will admit entrance. A village called Fairport has been laid out on the point below or east of the mouth of the river. Some houses are built, two taverns and three stores have been established, with a warehouse on the bank of the river. Preparations are making to form wharves, extending beyond the bar in such manner as to afford a harbor to vessels of any draft. If such work is completed, Fairport will be among the most flourishing villages on the south shore of Lake Erie. . . . Fairport has all the appearance of a commercial place, in infancy it must be confessed, but yet with such marks as will justify the anticipation of vigorous maturity."

Work was begun on Fairport's wharves soon after Darby's visit. A double row of timber posts were driven into the river bed by Ebenezer Hayes who owned and operated a pile driver. His son Russell rode a horse around and around a winch to furnish the power to raise the heavy weight. The two lines of posts were filled with stones to strengthen them against high waters. These posts did not prevent the sand bar from reforming, but did make a channel more easily dredgable.

Developing their harbor was begun by Fairport citizens, who were assisted in 1825 by a Congressional appropriation of $1,000 for "completing the pier at the mouth of the Grand River." This same year the brick lighthouse at Fairport, built under government contract, was finished. All was ready for increased traffic.

CANAL DAYS

More commerce did come to Fairport. In 1825 the Erie Canal opened from Buffalo to Albany, connecting Lake Erie with the Hudson River and eastern ports. Barges brought an increasing number of new residents, and returned east loaded with our produce. Wheat, wool, lumber, butter, lard, cheese, pork, tobacco and whiskey brought good prices in the New York market. Shipped west were luxury items, store goods which only the wealthiest citizens had been able to afford when transportation was by means of ox cart. An early freight list included clocks, tombstones and oysters. When the Ohio Canal connected Cleveland to the Ohio River in 1833, trade was opened with settlements down the Mississippi River to New Orleans. The real commercial development of Ohio began in these canal days when cheap and efficient water transportation reached into the rich interior farmlands.

The inland areas of the state not bordering the Ohio Canal were at a serious disadvantage and even before one canal was finished, a dozen more were being planned. On January 10, 1827 the state legislature passed a bill to make a canal "from some suitable point on the Ohio river, through the valley of the Mahoning river, to some suitable point on Lake Erie, or to some point on the Ohio Canal." For the next eight years one route after another was promoted by prominent citizens to favor their communities. Our own area proved to be no exception.

RICHMOND CITY

In 1832 Thomas Richmond, an eastern man on a journey through the Reserve, heard that land on the west bank at the mouth of Grand River was for sale and immediately bought it. He was a salt merchant and may well have been returning from an inspection of the Salt Tract in the Mahoning valley, learning there of the proposed Pennsylvania-Ohio canal. A man of considerable means and ability, Richmond soon developed a model community. He built a church, a school, a warehouse and dock. Business fell off in Fairport and gained in Richmond City.

In the meantime Richmond stirred up enthusiasm locally for the new canal. He talked with farmers along his prospective route from Fairport to Pittsburgh and tried to reach the ears of the legislators. However, his enterprise could not compete successfully with that of the well-established General Simon Perkins. Work on the cross-cut canal was begun in 1835 from Warren, Perkins' home, to meet the Ohio Canal at Akron, the center of Perkins' large land investments.

Grand River harbor was not to have canal boats added to the river boats, brigantines, schooners and wood-burning steamboats it was serving, but it nevertheless continued to be a busy spot. Merchants did a brisk business supplying the ships with food and fuel. Warehousemen unloaded and reloaded a variety of cargo. Taverns welcomed new settlers, most of whom were still coming from New England and New York State. However, the harbor had already received its first overseas immigrants.

THE MANX COME

In May 1826, William Tear sailed for Philadelphia from the Isle of Man, a small island in the Irish Sea between England and Ireland. Expecting to cross the Pennsylvania mountains by wagon to join two Manx families in Jefferson County, Ohio, Tear heard on shipboard of the newly opened Erie Canal and changed his plans. He took his family to New York and arranged passage to Albany. There, on the canal dock, they met Eliakim Field, owner of the Concord Iron Furnace, who was offering good inexpensive land near his furnace and cash paying jobs to anyone interested.

Tear took advantage of the offer and brought the first Manx family to our community. They were soon joined by more of their fellow-islanders who settled in Concord and nearby Leroy. The men worked at Field's or one of the other furnaces to pay for their farm land. Most of them had traded on the British mainland and spoke English as well as their native Gaelic tongue, but many of the women had to learn the new language. These newcomers soon became citizens, appreciating our democratic society as well as the opportunity to make a comfortable living.

The Manxmen proved to be a resolute people, outspoken and honest. Gaelic traditions, mingling with our New England heritage, brought enrichment to our growing world. That the Yankee settlements could so easily absorb this overseas group was a good omen for the future growth of what was to be Lake County.

To learn how we did become Lake County, Ohio, we must pick up the threads of our political development from the first days of settlement.

Chapter V

Liberty and Justice for All

When Connecticut's "reservation" of her western lands was accepted by the United States Congress, Connecticut became the sole owner and authority on the Western Reserve. Her General Assembly disposed of the soil, but did not provide the area with laws, courts or any form of government. The people of the Reserve were in much the same position as the early colonists. The seat of government was far away and neither group had any representation in its legislature. To obtain liberty and justice for all on the Reserve did not require a revolution, but it did take forethought and action over a number of years.

CONNECTICUT'S COLONY

From 1786 to 1796 there was no need for local government in an area peopled only by wandering hunters and traders. With the arrival of the surveyors, law and order were maintained by Cleaveland and Pease in their role as leaders of their parties and paymasters to nearly all the inhabitants.

For the following two years there was no authority. However, Arthur St. Clair, Governor of the Northwest Territory, assuming that he had the same jurisdiction over the Reserve as he had over the rest of the land lying north of the Ohio River, sent a tax collector to the district. This unfortunate man was greeted with laughter and ridicule. If taxes were to be paid, the settlers would pay them to their home state; but that state did not ask for taxes, much less set up courts to collect them.

Whittlesey, in his *Early History of Cleveland,* says that in these years "The people had no laws but those of God and their own consciences, yet they lived in great harmony. A bond of union existed in their common pleasures, as well as in their misfortunes. . . . Very few disputes occurred, such was the universal good feeling that prevailed."

This situation had of course a serious flaw. Men investing their money in land wanted written proof of their purchase. Few pioneers had time or means to make the long trip to Connecticut for a deed as Abbott, Paine and Walworth had done. On the other hand, the men who sold land on mortgage were equally interested in having proof of the money due them and a strong arm of law ready to see that it was collected. As the problem grew, both settlers and Connecticut Land Company shareholders petitioned the General Assembly for action. The obvious solution was to unite the Reserve with the nearest United States governmental authority, the Northwest Territory.

JOINING THE NORTHWEST TERRITORY

Organized by the Ordinance of 1787, the Northwest Territory covered the region out of which Ohio, Indiana, Illinois, Michigan, Wisconsin and part of Minnesota were eventually carved. The Ordinance, which was to influence all of United States' western expansion, described the stages of population growth each area must pass through to achieve statehood. It also included a Bill of Rights assuring freedom of worship, representative government, jury trial, guaranteeing private contracts, equal distribution of property between heirs and forbidding slavery.

To meet the demands for effective local government on the Western Reserve, three steps were taken. First, the United States Congress re-confirmed Connecticut's claim to the Reserve, thus guaranteeing our settlers' land titles. Next, Connecticut surrendered jurisdiction over the Reserve to the Federal Government. Congress then officially incorporated the Reserve into the Northwest Territory, and full authority was granted to Governor St. Clair. In 1800 he outlined the Reserve as a new county, named it Trumbull for the Governor of Connecticut, made Warren county seat, and appointed five judges to conduct county business.

TERRITORIAL TRUMBULL COUNTY

Lack of adequate facilities did not dampen our pioneers' enthusiasm for their new government. The first court session at Warren on August 25, 1800, was conducted — with great dignity — between two corn cribs. The judges, including Turhand Kirtland, presided over the business of the day. They appointed Justices of the Peace, among them Mentor's Moses Parks and Unionville's Aaron Wheeler; divided the county into eight townships, naming Charles Parker constable (the only township office) for "Payneville" Township; and chose the county officers.

Chosen by the Court as Sheriff of Trumbull County was David Abbott of Chagrin. Part of his responsibility was to suppress "all affrays, routs, riots, and insurrections," and he was authorized to call to his aid "the power of the county" if he needed it to maintain order.

Abbott also acted as county tax collector. On horseback through the forests from one settlement to another, his collection journeys were never uneventful. Sheriff Abbott, his saddlebags laden with silver and copper coins, met with numerous suspicious characters. Even hungry wild animals menaced his travels and at times harsh weather obscured the trails. He frequently suffered from cold and hunger or lost his way. His was a hard job, undertaken with a sense of civic responsibility which distinguishes Abbott as one of our early leaders.

FROM TERRITORY TO STATEHOOD

At first the only vote Trumbull County citizens had was for one Representative to the Territorial Legislature. On October 2, 1800, General Edward Paine was elected to this office by the forty-two voters who were able and willing to make the trip to Warren. For the next two years Paine worked side by side with the other legislators to bring more representative government to our citizens. Although Governor St. Clair was conservative and somewhat autocratic, the Legislature, following the rights guaranteed by the Ordinance of 1787, moved ahead toward statehood for the Ohio country.

In 1801 the judges named two election districts for Trumbull County and in October 1802 an election took place at Perkins Camp on Girdled Road in our present Concord Township. Samuel Huntington and David Abbott were sent to Ohio's Constitutional Convention. Meeting at Chillicothe, the convention began drawing plans to establish a new state. In less than a month Ohio's constitution was drafted and signed by the members.

On January 11, 1803, the people of Ohio elected their first Governor and legislature to take office in March. The Ohio country had become a state, the seventeeth to join the Union. Paine, Abbott and Huntington had all played important roles in this achievement.

TRUMBULL COUNTY, OHIO

In early elections, under both territorial and state government, qualified voters made their individual choice in an "audible voice," and their name and vote was recorded by two clerks of the election. Should a candidate resort to "bribery, threats, or treating with meat or drink" to sway a voter's choice, the candidate would disqualify himself from future elections for two years. Present to see that this rule was observed were three judges for the election, and to certify that these five officials had been true to their duties, a presiding judge signed the poll book.

Under state government, an established county could vote for its own county officers and the election districts were again reduced in area. Trumbull County Court set Ebenezer Merry's home at Marsh Settlement as voting place for Painesville Township in the county election of April

1803. The original poll book lists David Abbott, Ebenezer Merry and Anson Sessions as judges for the election. Edward Paine, Jr., and Abraham Tappen served as clerks, and presiding judge was Justice of the Peace Jesse Phelps. Thirty-four men gathered at Merry's to show their preference for William Rayen and Homer Hine, both of Youngstown, and David Hudson of Hudson as the three county commissioners. Five others — Oristes K. Hawley, Turhand Kirtland, Amos Spafford, David Abbott and Jesse Phelps — were unsuccessful candidates in the Painesville poll book record.

GEAUGA COUNTY IS FORMED

On December 31, 1805, an act was passed by the Ohio Legislature creating the county of Geauga, the act to take effect the following March 1. The new county included all of what now are Ashtabula, Cuyahoga (east of the river), Geauga and Lake Counties. New Market, on the bank of Grand River in Painesville Township, was named the principal seat of justice.

Captain Abraham Skinner's warehouse, the most substantial building in New Market, was used for the first Geauga County Courthouse. Named as Judges by the Ohio Legislature, Aaron Wheeler, John Walworth and Jesse Phelps called the court to order on March 4, 1806. They appointed the first officers for the new county. Edward Paine, Jr. became County Clerk, an office he held for twenty-five years, performing the duties done today by our Recorder and Clerk of Courts. Named also were Robert B. Parkman, Prosecuting Attorney; Joel Paine, Sheriff, and two County Commissioners, Nathaniel Doan and Oristes K. Hawley. Abraham Tappen, first serving as Surveyor, became the third County Commissioner in 1807.

FIRST GEAUGA COUNTY JAIL

One of the first actions of the Court of Common Pleas was to instruct the County Commissioners to build a jail for the county. This was the first official Geauga County building. The Commissioners: "did in March 1806 enter into an agreement with Abraham Skinner for to build of logs hewn on two sides, a house within the limits of the prison bounds as established by the court of Common Pleas, 12 x 14 feet on the ground, with two good log or plank floors, and one window with iron grates, with a good and sufficient chimney, and made in every other respect to the acceptance of the Commissioners and the Sheriff of said county. Said house to be completed on or before the first day of June next. Said Skinner on his part does agree to rent said house when built, to the Commissioners or their successors in office for a jail and to keep the same in sufficient repairs [without] any expense to the County, so long as they shall wish to employ it for a jail for the sum of fifteen dollars a year."

This sturdy building was not used frequently, although there is record of one man lashed as justifiable punishment for breaking the law. The early Court at New Market presided primarily over civil cases and ordered payment of fines in damage suits. According to tradition, the juries deliberated in the nearby woods.

THE COUNTY SEAT MOVES

In June of 1808 the Ohio Legislature appointed the Trumbull County Commissioners as an unbiased committee to locate the county seats for Geauga and the other counties the Legislature proposed to carve out of the original Trumbull: Cuyahoga, Ashtabula and Portage. The committee picked a centrally located spot in the then unbroken forest and agreed with the land owner, Peter Chardon Brooks, to name the new town Chardon in return for his gift of a park.

Several years were required to cut a road to the new location, to clear the park and build a courthouse. In the meantime, Henry Champion tried to have the county headquarters moved to his town. He wrote Samuel Huntington stressing the convenient location and offered to erect a building suitable for court sessions, school room and church meetings. His arguments were convincing and the town of Champion was named county seat in 1809.

During the next two years, Chagrin became part of new Cuyahoga County, and the County of Ashtabula was also established. On September 2, 1811, a sum of sixty dollars was appropriated by the Geauga Commissioners for the move to Chardon. The following spring Clerk Edward Paine, Jr. took the county records and his family to the new clearing. His simple cabin served as temporary office until a two-story hewn log building was completed. In the fall of 1813 the Geauga County Court met for the first time in the new Chardon Courthouse.

PAINESVILLE TOWNSHIP

Painesville Township, as it had been set up by the territorial Trumbull Court, included what are now the townships of Chardon, Hambden, Montville, Leroy, Concord, Perry, Mentor and Kirtland. Madison was in Richfield and Willoughby in Cleveland Township. As the population increased the need for more compact areas of government grew. One by one township organizations were formed and the order of their erection shows us something of the concentrations of population.

In 1806 Hambden's new government included today's Montville, Chardon and Leroy in its jurisdiction. In 1807 Harpersfield, including Unionville and Centerville, was set off from Richfield. In 1811 that part of Madison Township north of the Grand River was formed and received its present day name. In 1815 Mentor and Perry were taken from Painesville and Chagrin from Cleveland. Two years later Kirtland was carved from Mentor and in 1820 LeRoy (now spelt Leroy) was taken from Hambden. Concord, the last to form a township government, left Painesville in 1822.

We have no early records of Painesville government* but when Governor St. Clair permitted the first election of township officials in 1802, Cleveland's government included the following officers: Chairman, Town Clerk, three Trustees, two Appraisers of Houses, a Lister, three Supervisors of Highways, two Overseers of the Poor, two Fence Viewers and two Constables. It is obvious that an area had to contain at least seventeen able-bodied white men over twenty-one before a township could be formed!

COUNTY DISSATISFACTION

Chardon seemed an ideal location for the county seat. With its fine hilltop location, it was almost the geographical center and not far from being the population center of Geauga. However, after 1815 many more settlers came to the northern townships. By 1820 Painesville with 1,257 residents was the largest township on the Reserve. Her citizens wanted the prestige of a courthouse and could claim their location would serve more people more conveniently. Agitation grew for two decades. Suggestions were made, first for moving the county seat, then, for a division of the county. Chardon residents opposed either idea.

On May 16, 1839, Dr. Storm Rosa, Editor of the *Telegraph,* summed up the arguments on both sides. He wrote: "In forming our opinion of a measure of such vital importance, as a removal of a seat of justice from one portion of the county to another, we should be guided with an eye single to the public good. . . . this much is certain, that a large majority of the people of Geauga County have explicitly expressed their decided disapprobation to any interference with the original policy of the county in establishing the seat of justice at Chardon.

"Division of the county has been suggested as less objectional to the people and one which will remedy the inconvenience of the present location to the inhabitants of the north and be satisfactory to those of the south. The only objection to the division of the county which can be argued with any plausibility is the increased expenditures in erecting

---

*The only known copy of Painesville's first election is in the Parmly House corner stone.

new buildings and paying of county officers. . . . The first of these objections cannot be argued by the south inasmuch as the county buildings
will remain theirs and will consequently be no further removed from
them than they are now. The next objection may be argued with some
degree of plausibility — the officers of each county must be paid re-
spectively; but it must be kept in mind that we have but one salary
officer, and the remainder are paid *per diem*. And again the south
country would be relieved of at least two thirds of their taxation for
criminal prosecutions: the conclusion is, then, that no good argument
can be used by the south against the division of the county.

"We are told that great unanimity prevails among the people of the
north part of the county and that with all the objections which can be
urged they are still for a division of the county."

A week later a letter to the editor from An Old Resident of Painesville added, "We once belonged to the county of Trumbull. The changes
of a newly settled country, the rapid increase of population and business, made it expedient to divide. Whoever heard the people of Warren
complain that their vested rights were taken away from them, when
other counties were established? . . . . Yet that people understand the
value of office and money as well as any other."

LAKE COUNTY IS ESTABLISHED

On October 22, 1839, the *Telegraph* contained the following: "Notice is thereby given, that application will be made to the next General
Assembly of the state of Ohio, for the erection of a new County, to
consist of the Townships of Kirtland, Concord, LeRoy, that part of
Thompson north of No. ten [survey line], Madison, Perry, Painesville,
Mentor, Willoughby (in the county of Cuyahoga) and that portion of
the State of Ohio, lying north of the five last mentioned Townships,
with the county seat in the Township of Painesville." The notice was
signed by leading citizens of all the townships. Claiming ownership of
Lake Erie to the International Boundary had been necessary to meet the
state requirement for acreage.

Benjamin Bissell, our State Senator, followed the bill for the erection of the new county through the proper legislative channels, and on
March 20, 1840, Lake County was established, with election of officers
set for April 6. The jubilant Painesville citizens privately collected
$5,000 for a new courthouse even before a formal committee could be
appointed. Political party meetings were called and slates of officers
were made up. On April 9 the *Telegraph* headlined the news: "LAKE
COUNTY ELECTION, Splendid Whig Victory."

Lake County, Ohio, was in business.

Chapter VI

The Wilderness Retreats

A typical frontiersman of the Reserve did not trudge the western trails to escape civilization. His aim, beyond making a better home for his family, was to extend the patterns of a society he had temporarily left, to transplant the neat and well-conducted New England towns he had known.

Law and order were acknowledged necessities and were soon provided. Basic routes of transportation and communication were blazed through the forests. Government and roads drew our people together into social groups and rekindled interest in other advantages of civilization. Educated professional men came to serve our communities. Intellectual stimulus was provided by libraries, newspapers, innovations in architecture, musical groups and exposure to art. Schools and churches were organized and our communities also witnessed a new religion's growth in the Kirtland hills. Gradually culture conquered the wilderness.

PROFESSIONAL MEN

Our early settlers wanted the benefits of town life brought into the pioneer villages as rapidly as possible. They welcomed the first professional men, who soon established fine reputations in their fields as well as in the communities they served.

Tappen and Abbott were among the first lawyers admitted to the Trumbull County bar. Huntington started his practice in Geauga County in 1810, and in 1824 William L. Perkins arrived in Painesville.

In Connecticut, Perkins had read his father's law books, working through the complicated language and finding the cases fascinating problems. He was not a sturdy boy and his family felt that preparatory school and college would be too hard for him. To improve his health he went to work on a farm. He studied in the evenings and became a school teacher when he was twenty-one. For another two years he read law in the office of a local attorney, then set out for the Western Reserve to begin his career.

Perkins brought with him the New England attitude that law was the most learned profession, dependent on a liberal education, precise training and high moral character. He was fond of saying, "Though almost all books are worth reading, few are worth studying, and of these few the largest and best English Dictionary is the most valuable." With this conviction, Mr. Perkins helped place the legal profession and our courts in a respected position.

MEDICINE

Life on the edge of the wilderness was a constant struggle against nature's elements, bodily ills and the threat of death. Chills and fevers, or afflictions of the lungs and digestive organs were very common. Malaria flourished in poorly drained areas. Tuberculosis took a heavy toll of life, and lack of proper sanitation spread disease. Popular home remedies were concoctions of snakeroot, catnip, pennyroyal, peppermint, tansy, turpentine, saffron and slippery elm. Doctors were usually summoned only when such remedies failed to bring improvement or when an accident was too serious for the elementary treatment of an untrained layman.

Only a small minority of Ohio's early doctors had even attended a series of lectures at a medical school, and a much smaller number were graduates. A typical medical student worked with a local practitioner, mixing powders and rolling pills, reading from his books and accompanying him on his visits. This period of apprenticeship lasted about three years, then the new physician was ready to start his own practice.

We were fortunate in having well-trained and scholarly men in our early communities. Dr. John M. Henderson came to Chagrin in 1813 and Dr. John H. Mathews to Painesville in 1814. Dr. Storm Rosa first settled in Centerville, but moved after two years to Painesville in 1818. Dr. George W. Card settled in Chagrin the following year. Drs. Andrews Merriman and Edward Plympton came soon after to Centerville, and Dr. Medad P. Sherwood made Unionville his home.

Our first doctors in Lake County not only ministered to the ills of the people but also served their communities in other ways. Recognizing the need for more well trained physicians on the Reserve, Dr. Card and Dr. Henderson were prime movers in the organization of a Medical College at Chagrin. Dr. Rosa was editor of the *Telegraph* for a short time and served as first president of the Painesville Education Society. These men shared their education with their neighbors.

THE PARMLY FAMILY, DENTISTS

When the Parmly family came to Perry in 1817, two of the sons, Levi and Eleazer, had already set out to make their mark in what was then an undeveloped trade — dentistry. After three years apprenticeship to an English dentist in Boston, Levi started his practice in Montreal. He went to lecture in London for the years 1817 and 1818, then settling in New Orleans for thirty years, he wrote a number of publications on dental hygiene.

Eleazer received most of his training from his older brother and chose New York City as his home. In 1834 he was the first president of the Society of Surgeon Dentists of the City and State of New York, in 1840 one of the founders of the American Society of Dental Surgeons and received from this organization one of the original degrees of D.D.S. He married well and his wealth and social position added much prestige to the new profession.

Jahiel Parmly worked on his father's farm for three years and then joined his older brothers for training. For thirty years he undertook professional trips through the South, coming back to Perry for the summers. It is said he returned "as thin as a June shad, but plentifully supplied with the coin of the realm." He was probably the most successful itinerant dentist in history.

Samuel, the youngest brother, studied with Eleazer and settled in New York. The oldest brother, David, remained a Perry farmer, but with cousins, brothers-in-law and sons, the Parmly family produced eighteen dentists in two generations. Of these Jahiel remained most closely associated with Lake County. It was, however, Eleazer who built the Parmly Hotel, Painesville, in 1861, and Samuel returned frequently for the summer. Levi had strong affection for the family home and though he died in France, by his request he was buried on the family lot in Perry.

LIBRARIES

Few of the early pioneers found room among their household goods to bring books on their western trip. However, the traditions of New England, the love of reading and respect for the world of ideas could not be forgotten.

In 1819 the Mentor Library Company was organized with twenty-five hundred shares at $2.50 each. Thirty-six subscribers from our present Willoughby, Kirtland, Chester, Concord and Painesville, as well as Mentor, contributed to its funds. Who traveled east to purchase the books is now forgotten, but the library offered a variety of history, biography and astronomy, with a few novels and essays for lighter reading. Mentor Library Company served its subscribers for forty years.

In the meantime, the Franklin Library was organized in Chagrin, and Painesville formed a Library Association. In 1824 there was a notice in the *Telegraph* that this Association would sell its books at auction. In the same issue notice was given for all in favor of forming a new library to meet in the school house. This was the method used when a group of subscribers had read all the collection. These early libraries were organized for their own membership. The idea of free public libraries was not to develop until much later in the century.

ARCHITECTURE

In 1811 there came to Painesville a man who has left our county a great treasure of beauty. Jonathan Goldsmith was born in 1783 in New Haven, Connecticut. His father, a ship captain, died at sea of small pox and Jonathan, at age eleven, was bound out to a shoemaker. Six years later he was able to buy out the balance of his time and apprentice himself to a carpenter until he was twenty-one. With what little he earned at this trade he borrowed and purchased books on architecture. With determination and an ardent love for his new craft, he spelled his way through them and absorbed both knowledge and taste. After he proved his skill in Hinsdale, Massachusetts, and found a wife there, he came to the Reserve.

For seven years the family worked to clear their land and make a prosperous farm. In 1818, Goldsmith replaced his original log cabin with a farm house of unique design. This house brought something new to the Reserve: the Greek Revival style of architecture.

When sawmills were built the pioneers replaced their log cabins with frame houses similar to those they had known in New England. (see the Walworth-Huntington house) Just beyond Unionville in Ashtabula County there is one of these early clapboard houses, Shandy Hall, built by the Harper family. Their home, a simple story-and-a-half dwelling, is a museum today and one well worth visiting. Another museum, Dunham Tavern, 6709 Euclid Avenue, Cleveland, is an example of an early two-story clapboard building. These out-of-the-county homes are important because their original lines have not been altered and their interiors can be examined. They are the colonial architecture of Connecticut transplanted to the Western Reserve which Goldsmith was to change.

THE GREEK REVIVAL

In the late 1700's, Thomas Jefferson was among the many influential thinkers in our country who believed that the ideals of our new republic related more to the political philosophy of ancient Greece than to any other civilization. Gradually interest in all phases of this culture grew from the Atlantic seaboard to the Reserve. Evidence of this interest remains for us today in the names of Euclid Avenue, honoring the Greek mathematician, and Mentor, commemorating the tutor of Ulysses' son.

It followed that there was considerable interest in Greek architecture and study of how best to adapt its classic forms to the buildings of a new country. Goldsmith carried the thought to the Reserve that the fine home could be patterned after a temple. Though he did not confine himself to this style alone, it is for these buildings that he is most famous. These designs turned the home so that the gable end faced the road. The exterior was finished with flush boards, rather than clapboard, resulting in a smooth white surface that gave the appearance of stone. When pilasters, or flat columns, were added the effect achieved was that of a Greek temple.

Within this general scheme Goldsmith developed unique and now famous designs considered to be the best of the American Greek Revival. Set at one side, the door opened into a hallway with graceful stairs rising to the second story. The doorway was crowned with a long shallow transom and framed with vertical windows on either side. In the gable was a distinctive fanlight. Fortunately, some of the many houses Goldsmith built between 1818 and his death in 1847 are still standing for us to enjoy and admire. (See Mathews House)

NEWSPAPERS

While Goldsmith was transforming our villages, a young man named Eber Howe was informing them by riding through our countryside once a week delivering *The Cleveland Herald* to its sixty eastern subscribers. Painesville appeared to Howe as a much more vigorous community than Cleveland, not yet touched off to growth by the Ohio canal. It is said that Goldsmith's encouragement decided Howe to leave his Cleveland partner and found *The Painesville Telegraph*.

The first issue, a four column sheet with five advertisers and a list of one hundred and fifty subscribers, came out in 1822. By the time Howe sold the *Telegraph* in 1835, the paper was well established. Warren's *Trump of Fame, The Cleveland Register* and *The Cleveland Herald* antedate it, but they have long since disappeared. The *Telegraph* remains the oldest surviving newspaper on the Reserve.

Howe was one of the early editors to concern himself with local news and to take a firm stand on local issues. His *Mormanism Unvailed* [sic], published in 1834, was the first book in the long controversy over Mormon beliefs and behavior. Howe was a vigorous abolitionist and not only spoke against slavery but aided escaped slaves. He is also given credit for introducing a new word into our language, a word that came from a local incident which he relates in his *Autobiography and Recollections*. A group of counterfeiters were discovered in Painesville and their machine was "a great wonderment for some time among the crowd that had collected around. . . . Many remarks and suggestions were made as to the name it bore or the one which should be given it. . . . Finally someone called it a 'Bogus'." The word "bogus" twice appeared in the *Telegraph* in 1827 as a description for the fraudulent operations of counterfeiting, and it has remained in our vocabulary with much of its original meaning.

When he left the *Telegraph* Eber Howe started a woolen mill in Concord, proving himself as successful a businessman as journalist. He continued an influential citizen in our county until his death in 1884.

MUSIC

Music played an important role in the social life of our pioneer settlements. We remember the fife-and-drum band at John Walworth's Fourth of July celebration in 1801. We can imagine again Mrs. Alexander Harper singing to her guests at her party the following year. Obviously, the pleasures of music enhanced the pleasures of companionship.

Joseph Talcott conducted an evening group in Madison's Block House School in 1815. He read the lyrics and sang the music from his one song book, and his pupils memorized and followed him as best they could. Of the songs they sang, rounds were most popular because, it was reported, "it gave the singers great satisfaction to go off on separate ways and then come together in tone and harmony."

Mentor also had an early singing school which performed many selections including church music. Their regular closing hymn was a spirited rendition of "Blow, ye, the trumpet, blow" and one young man, so the story is told, found this an ideal opportunity for some fun. He climbed the roof with a big tin horn under his arm and waited through the evening. At the first "Blow, ye," *he* blew, pointing his horn down the chimney. Everyone ran out of the cabin thinking the angel Gabriel had surely come, only to find their impish neighbor astride the ridgepole!

By 1819 Madison could boast the first band in the county, although we have no details of instruments represented. Singing, of course, was easier to perform as each participant carried his own instrument with him. Whatever the method, making music was a wonderful excuse for getting together and provided the early settlements with much entertainment.

ART

Although our early pioneers welcomed books and newspapers, adopted new ideas of architecture, and enjoyed music, they did not show much interest in art. Dan Beard in *Hardly a Man is Now Alive* tells about his artist father, James H. Beard: "My father was inspired to become an artist after watching a man sketch the design for a figurehead of the ship *Walk-in-the-Water*, the first steamboat on Lake Erie, launched [at Buffalo] in 1818. There were no art schools, there were no artists anywhere in the neighborhood, so he made himself brushes of the fur of wild animals. He made himself a pestle and stone for grinding his own colors. He mixed them with oil, and, there being no such thing in those days as a paint tube, he used fish bladders for that purpose, filling them with his paints. He made his own stretchers, stretched and sized his own canvas, and started to paint some truly modernistic pictures. But in the little village of Painesville art was not appreciated, so he, like his father before him, started out on a hike to seek his fortune. Choosing Pittsburgh as his first port, he worked as a keelboatman down to Cincinnati, where he began his art career, about 1834."

James H. Beard eventually became a popular portrait painter. His subjects included such men as Henry Clay, John Quincy Adams, and Zachary Taylor. Beard painted a picture of a child with his dog, which was so admired that many parents besieged him to paint their children with their pets. He turned his efforts to animals and became famous for his skill in depicting them.

William H. Beard, born in Painesville, followed his brother to Cincinnati to draw humorous pictures of bears and other animals, many of them used as cartoons in the leading magazines of the day. Both men returned to Painesville frequently to visit their mother and James brought his family back to live for several years. Although Painesville did not purchase his paintings, it had to be impressed by his personality. Dan wrote, "My father was six feet tall and straight as an Indian. He wore a soft linen cambric shirt with full front and a wide Byron collar. His large neck-handkerchiefs were folded and tied in loose, flowing bows; his hair was worn parted in the middle and it hung in rich brown curls on his shoulders, all of which produced a striking resemblance to the portraits of Albrecht Durer."

An artist was in our midst and our world was enlarged.

Chapter VII

The Three R's — and More

One of the cornerstones of our pioneers' New England heritage was an appreciation for education, and many of our early men were well-educated people. Moses Cleaveland was a Yale graduate. Members of his surveying party knew the fundamentals of mathematics and kept journals recording their adventures. David Abbott had had an advanced education, was a thinker and a planner. John Walworth of Painesville had more than an average background of formal schooling. On the list of our first school teachers are familiar pioneer names: Crary of Kirtland, Paine, Huntington, Wheeler of Unionville and Abraham Tappen.

OUR FIRST SCHOOL TEACHER

Abraham Tappen came to the Western Reserve in 1801 with John Walworth's supply party. He was an educated young man with character and ability. His first years here he served as agent for the Connecticut Land Company. Tappen helped General Paine lay out the Chillicothe Road, surveyed the Reserve west of the Cuyahoga in 1808, became postmaster at Unionville and later served seven years as Associate Judge of Geauga County Court of Common Pleas.

In our early history, Tappen is best remembered as our first school teacher. The winter after he arrived he taught in a small log cabin on the bank of Grand River, collecting together a dozen pupils from the Paine and Walworth families. In a single brief school term he taught reading, 'riting and 'rithmetic.

EARLY SCHOOLS

The "Three R's" were the essentials the pioneer farmer agreed were useful to his sons, for a little learning came in handy at market. If a girl learned to read, her mother usually taught her from the family Bible. In the early days, a man was too concerned with making a home in the wilderness to give much thought to his children's "book-learning." He needed the help of all his family and there were few minutes left for study. Ten years passed after Abraham Tappen's class before further formal teaching started in this region. In these ten years the greater hazards of frontier life were conquered and time, teachers and students became available.

In 1811 Miss Kate Smith of Euclid taught in a Mentor log cabin for 75c a week, supplementing her earnings by spinning flax as the children did their lessons. The following year Experience Dewey taught in a larger cabin, which burned during the winter and with it the few precious books collected for the children.

In 1812 a two-story frame building was built on the southeast corner of the park in Painesville. The first floor was used for a school weekdays and for a church on Sundays. The second floor served as the Masonic Lodge. Franklin Paine, who had come home disabled from the War of 1812 and unable to work in the fields, was the first schoolmaster here.

The next year Mary Crary of Kirtland taught a class in Madison Township, and Aaron Wheeler served as teacher to Unionville's school which opened in 1814. These classes encouraged the citizens of Centerville to erect a substantial cabin of square logs on the park. This building was known for years as the Block House School. It, like Painesville's building, served also as a community center for church services and social gatherings.

In Kirtland, Estelle Crary held the first classes in 1814, and five years later the village built a frame schoolhouse in the Flats. Also in 1814, Leroy united with Thompson to erect a log school near their joint township line. Lovinia Hulburt was the first teacher here. The next year schools were opened in Perry and Concord.

TEACHERS AND SCHOOL TERMS

Young lady teachers, who had had some schooling in the east, earned 75c to a $1.00 a week, plus board and lodging. Each family with children in school took turns boarding the teacher. She seldom collected her wages in cash. Mary Smith taught at the Block House School one year and received a calf and a bureau. One man paid a load of corn, another man took it to Painesville and exchanged it for linen flax, which in turn a woman wove into a bedspread for Mary. Thus three more school bills were paid.

Young men who were anxious to further their education found teaching in winter a way of earning money for their college tuition. They usually received $10 a month plus board. A teacher was chosen not so much for his knowledge but because he had free time and wanted a job.

He was employed if he could read the Bible without stumbling, write "a decent copy," do a few sums, and mend the quill pens which the students used with homemade ink when paper was available.

For a school term of three winter months, the schoolmaster kept order in the one room schoolhouse from 9:00 to 4:00 six days a week. At the end of the day, he mended the quills, swept out the mud and crumbs and banked the fire in the big open fireplace to keep a few coals hot until morning. Then he was free to make his way to that week's home.

INSIDE A SCHOOLHOUSE

The students were usually graded by their ability to read from a few text books on hand. A description of a school in 1822 says that, "The first class were those in the *English Reader,* the second in the *American Preceptor*, the third in the *New Testament*, the fourth in Webster's *Spelling Book.* We read all around, class by class, before recess; and after, we read again and spelled, standing on the floor. It was a great honor to be at the head and keep there three or four days running." The author goes on to say that he had neither grammar nor geography and that there was no such thing as an arithmetic class. Each pupil worked independently with whatever book he had. When he could not do a problem, he asked help from the teacher, who was often as puzzled as he.

The schoolmaster had three methods of keeping order in those days. A wriggling child was set to writing on his slate or with his quill pen such adages as "Contentment is a Virtue," "Honesty is the best Policy," "A penny saved is a penny earned." For the boy whose thoughts were out hunting rabbits, there was a high stool near the master's desk and a dunce's cap. For the unruly, there was a bundle of switches. "Spare the rod and you spoil the child" was firmly believed by parents and teachers alike. Children of all ages, even boys as big as the teacher, in a single room must certainly have exercised the teacher's ingenuity in matters of discipline.

There could be other disturbing episodes for a teacher too. Rachel Terry, who taught an early school in Mentor, told her grandchildren that the Indians used to look in and see her quiet class, so odd to them, and let out a war whoop — to liven things up a little. She said she didn't scare easily, but trying to settle the class back to work must have taken a real effort. Mary Crary, on her way home from school one evening heard a noise behind her and turned to face a bear. Terrified, she used the only weapon which she had — her umbrella. She opened and closed it rapidly, pointing it at the bear's nose. The animal thought better of his interest in the young lady and fled. Mary escaped in the opposite direction.

INFLUENCE OF F. J. HUNTINGTON

Into this rather haphazard educational life arrived in 1816 a young man who was to leave a distinct mark on the community. Flavius Josephus Huntington came to Painesville at the suggestion of his uncle, Governor Huntington, and devoted over thirty years to instructing our children. He had had a fine education and had been an assistant in Connecticut's well-known New London Grammar School. Besides experience, he brought a warm understanding of human nature, excellent personal habits and conscientious concern for education and the development of character. He was remembered by his many pupils as kind and gentle, precise and painstaking, strict yet patient. He influenced three generations of students, and led in the establishment of a sound and stable educational system for our county.

THE FIRST HIGH SCHOOL

In March 1823, an announcement appeared in the *Telegraph*: "The Painesville Academy is now open with Mr. George Thompson as tutor in the following branches: English, Latin, Greek, Elements of Rhetoric and Natural Philosophy. The terms of tuition are $3 a quarter." Although this early private high school did not thrive, it was the forerunner of a Painesville Education Society, incorporated in 1831, with Dr. Storm Rosa as president. Eleven directors included eight Painesville citizens, William Graham of Perry, Lewis Dilley of Concord and Daniel Kerr of Mentor. A building was erected on Painesville's Washington Street, and for twenty years the reorganized Academy flourished. It drew students from all our townships as well as from neighboring areas.

A TEACHERS' SEMINARY FOR KIRTLAND

On September 1, 1838, the Reverend Nelson Slater opened the Western Reserve Teachers' Seminary in Kirtland, using the deserted Mormon Temple and nearby empty houses for its campus. The Seminary advertized competent teachers and facilities for two or three hundred students.

Their school year was divided into three terms. "The fall term will close in time for young gentlemen to teach winter schools; the winter term in time for young Ladies to teach summer schools, and the summer term about the commencement of haying and harvesting." Tuition for the three terms was $18, with an additional charge of $1 to $1.50 per week for board and room. In order to qualify for admission, "students, unless advanced in their studies, must have attained the age of fourteen years."

For nearly twenty years, under the direction of Slater, followed by Dr. Asa Lord and Dr. John Nichols, this early normal school maintained high standards and graduated well-trained teachers. It furnished Lake County with educated schoolmasters, and sent graduates to all parts of the state. Kirtland Seminary helped spread the reputation of the Western Reserve for devotion to the ideals of education.

A NEW COLLEGE AND A NEW NAME

Chagrin also wanted an institution for advanced study. There were already two liberal arts colleges not far away, Western Reserve then at Hudson and the Institute at Oberlin, both attracting some students from Lake County. Men planned a college for Chagrin that would offer training in a different field but one vital to the life of the communities.

Among those interested were two physicians, Dr. John M. Henderson and Dr. George W. Card. They had attended Fairfield Medical School in central New York State and felt that as the only such college in Ohio was in Cincinnati three hundred miles away, Chagrin would contribute much by organizing one. Plans were set in motion to establish a medical school on the Reserve.

The president of Fairfield Medical School, Dr. Westel Willoughby, Jr., was much admired by his former students. They agreed that his name would add prestige to the new institution and help attract teachers and students. There was also hope that Dr. Willoughby, a man of considerable wealth, might give financial support to the school. In the fall of 1834 Willoughby University of Lake Erie was incorporated, and the name Willoughby appeared on our maps.

From an uncertain start that first November, the school went on to build an imposing three-story brick building in 1836. The quality of the faculty improved. One of the fine physicians to join the staff was Dr. Daniel Peixotto, our first recorded Jewish resident. Born in the West Indies, he was a doctor of acknowledged learning and ability in New York before he came to the Reserve. He was described as "an elegant classic scholar, an eloquent writer and lecturer, and whether on literature, history or the healing art, always interesting." He became one of the most skillful surgeons in the country.

By 1842 Willoughby citizens felt they had a permanent institution; but some of the professors, including Dr. Peixotto, began to consider Cleveland, now thriving with Ohio Canal trade, a better site. The next year four of the most capable doctors applied to Western Reserve College for permission to form a new faculty.

One of the men drawn to Cleveland was Turhand Kirtland's son, Dr. Jared Potter Kirtland. A graduate of Yale Medical School and experienced with practice in Connecticut, he had come to Ohio in 1823, settling on Cleveland's west side in 1837. He became one of the great intellectual leaders of his day. He was physician, teacher, editor, philosopher, scientist and horticulturist. Kirtland Hills honors the name of Jared Potter Kirtland for his pioneer leadership in the natural sciences.

For three or four years Willoughby Medical College struggled on, but there was little need for two competing schools only twenty miles apart and the last graduation at Willoughby was January 26, 1847. The next year the remaining faculty and students moved to Columbus, organizing Starling Medical College which eventually became the Medical School of Ohio State University.

MORE SCHOOLS ARE ESTABLISHED

When Willoughby Medical College disbanded, it left behind a sturdy school building and a group of citizens still interested in having an institution for higher education. With help from these people in remodeling and refurnishing the building, and with support from the Presbyterian Society, Willoughby Female Seminary was established in 1847. The Reverend Alvan Nash served as principal. On the faculty were accomplished lady scholars, many of them graduates of Mount Holyoke Seminary in Massachusetts. The new Willoughby school was very successful and attracted pupils from far and near.

Tragedy struck the school however one February morning in 1856 when a fire destroyed the recitation building. Painesville citizens quickly offered to help the staff of the school. This encouragement and the prospect of increased financial aid drew the Seminary to the county seat. Painesville's new school was eventually to become Lake Erie College.

Willoughby residents still wanted a school for their community. Local Methodists urged a co-educational seminary, and the idea was generally approved. The Reverend Benjamin Excell assisted in raising the $12,000 needed for a new building. Willoughby Collegiate Institution opened its doors in 1859 with one hundred eighty-three students. Providing high school and college training to many young people until 1882, it was then taken over by the town's Board of Education for a public high school.

Madison also had its private Seminary which offered higher education to the eastern part of the county. Opened in 1847, it grew and prospered until, like Willoughby's institution, public schools were organized. One of Madison Seminary's buildings still stands on Middle Ridge Road after many years service as a home for Civil War army nurses and soldiers' widows.

OUR PUBLIC SCHOOL SYSTEM

An ideal of state-supported and state-supervised public schools was talked about in Ohio as early as 1820. The first effective step toward this goal became known as the Akron Law, enacted in 1847. This law allowed (but did not compel) cities and incorporated towns to organize special school districts into systems of graded schools. A few years later another law authorized a state tax, to be levied for the benefit of public schools, and created the office of an elected state commissioner of education.

During this formative period a statewide teachers' association was organized. Dr. Asa Lord, former principal of the Western Reserve Teachers' Seminary in Kirtland, became the editor of *The Journal of Education*, the association's official magazine. His leadership helped raise the level of the profession and spurred further progress in the system. Through Dr. Lord's influence, Lake County took a major part in the development of Ohio's public schools.

In July of 1851, Dr. Lord talked in Painesville, stirring the community to take advantage of the new opportunities, and a Board of Education was elected that fall. The one-room schools already had been receiving some neighborhood tax support so that it was not difficult to arrange a townwide tax to support the consolidated administration. The next job to be done was to reorganize the students into graded classes. The Board then took over the Painesville Academy in order to establish a free high school. The Public Schools of Painesville opened in 1852 with five hundred students and ten teachers.

Our modern school system had begun.

Chapter VIII

We Gather Together

Churches grew on the Reserve much as schools did, slowly at first, and then with added momentum as the scattered settlements became villages. There were three difficulties facing organized religion. The early settlers were first concerned with food and shelter, with carving a farm out of the forest and building a decent home. Men were far too occupied in their struggle with nature to give up one day out of seven for the Sabbath. These New Englanders had come from communities where a whole day was devoted to religion. Their attendance had been expected at morning and afternoon service, and an evening service was often added. Such a day was out of the question in a frontier world.

Secondly, many of our people had come west with the desire to escape New England's church taxes levied on them — whatever their belief — in many towns. These men were tired of the strict puritanical restraints of their ancestors, and saw no reason to subject themselves to the dictates of a minister.

In the third place, the pattern of settlement of the Reserve did not immediately form villages with enough people to support a minister. Lots were sold as each stockholder of the Connecticut Land Company could find a buyer. Clearings were scattered, and any religious instruction, like the rudiments of education, had to be provided within the immediate family circle.

Efforts to bring organized religion to the frontier became effective as these difficulties diminished. First came the itinerant preachers or circuit riders. Earliest on the scene were representatives of the Connecticut Missionary Society, a cooperative group from the Congregational and Presbyterian Churches. One of the Society's most dedicated riders, the Reverend Joseph Badger, left an account of his experiences. His journal ruefully reflects his encounters with our early settlers' initial indifference to organized religion, but he does give an interesting description of life on this frontier.

THE REVEREND JOSEPH BADGER

In July of 1801, the Reverend Badger started from Warren to make a tour of the Western Reserve. He wrote in his diary, "On Monday I returned to Aurora, from which I took the only road from the south to the Lake; got very wet in a thunder shower. Arrived at Newburg before dark. In this place were five families. Preached here on the Sabbath; on Monday visited Cleveland, in which there were only two families. Here I fell in company with Judge [Turhand] Kirtland. We rode from here to Painesville; found on the way, in Euclid, one family; in Chagrin one; in Mentor four and in Painesville two families. Next day we rode to Burton, preached on the Sabbath, and visited the families in this place. From this I found my way to Austinburg. In this place were ten families, and about the same number in Harpersfield. Thus were preached to all the families on the Reserve. . . ."

The next year, "On the last week in July, 1802, I set out; reached Painesville on Saturday. Sabbath preached to about twenty, consisting of two families and several workmen; not one seemed to have the least regard for the Sabbath; I was, however, treated decently. Monday rode on to a small settlement of five families, in a place called the 'Marsh,' in Mentor, and preached a lecture; and next day called on Mr. Abbott, at Chagrin, who appeared very inimical to the cause of missions; and said he did not thank the Missionary Society for sending missionaries out here."

Badger arrived, on his circuit, at Perkins Camp in time for the election, October, 1802. He was invited to eat with the men, but in utter dismay he saw them seat themselves and begin eating immediately. In firm tones of indignation, the Reverend Badger announced, "Gentlemen, if you will attend with Christian decency until the blessing of God is asked on this provision, I will sit down with you, otherwise I can not!" The men recalled their spiritual obligations and laid down their knives and forks while the Reverend asked the blessing.

That winter Badger was again at General Paine's house. "On Monday having crossed the Grand River on a shallow rapid, I proceeded on to Marsh Settlement; and from thence to the Chagrin. Here I found the river completely blocked up with ice, and now it was near night. I returned three miles, and tarried with a family exceedingly hardened against any religious instruction." The Reverend Badger had greater success in Austinburg and did organize a church there before he went further west to work with the Indians. He returned, helped organize the church in Madison and later served a church in Kirtland for a few years. Struggling with hardships and discouragements, he spent his life working devotedly for the cause nearest his heart.

CONNECTICUT MISSIONARY SOCIETY CHURCHES

Other missionaries came to the Reserve and more settlers arrived, some with stronger church affiliations, some just homesick for the familiar ways of New England. As the communities grew, people came to realize the importance of religious organization. To most of them the church was also a symbol of education and refinement. The next missionaries to arrive on the scene were welcomed more cordially and Connecticut Missionary Society preachers helped form permanent churches.

On Sunday, June 17, 1810, thirteen persons met in the Geauga County Courthouse on the Painesville park. Under the leadership of the Society's Reverend Nathan Darrow, a church was "gathered, constituted and organized." Darrow's circuit was a large one, and he could come only once a month to conduct services, but the First Church grew nonetheless. In the early years, Congregational and Presbyterian policies were intermixed, but in 1862 the members voted to become a Congregational Church, and so it has remained.

Several Unionville settlers invited the Reverend Giles Cowles of Austinburg to preach to them, which he did in June, 1813. However, Cowles was not pleasing to everyone in the community. Tappen and the Harpers claimed he was a Federalist in politics and refused to hear him speak. The following summer Cowles, Badger and the Reverend Jonathan Leslie were able to form a church of nine members in Centerville, with services held regularly in the Block House School.

On September 3, 1819, a group gathered in the home of Levi Smith in Kirtland "to consult as to the propriety of having a church organized" and in 1822 this congregation built a log cabin on the site of Kirtland's Old South Church. The Chagrin Church, organized by the Connecticut Missionary Society in 1833, followed the Presbyterian creed and is the oldest group in the county today of that faith.

METHODIST CHURCHES — IRA EDDY

In the meantime, other missions were interested in bringing the word of God to the Western Reserve. From the Methodist Episcopal Church came the Reverend Ira Eddy to preach the gospel to the pioneers. With his eloquence and enthusiasm he gathered together many small groups. Frontier farmers liked the colorful drama with which he called them to turn away from their sins. He brought excitement into their hardworking lonely lives, and they responded to him. In five active years from 1816 to 1821, Eddy organized Methodist Churches in Mentor, Chagrin, Concord, Painesville, Kirtland and Wickliffe.

Eddy carried his library with him on his one faithful companion, his horse. Like other circuit riders for the Methodist Church, he usually rode ten miles or more a day, preached every day and twice on Sundays. He endured great hardships on his long rides over our rough roads, often no more than forest trails. One day he rode from Chagrin, following the river south, for an evening meeting at Bainbridge. When darkness

HOME OF JOHN WALWORTH AND LATER SAMUEL HUNTINGTON

JOHN WALWORTH
Courtesy of Mrs. Eugene Izant

SAMUEL HUNTINGTON
From a painting by C. L. Ransom
in the state capitol, Columbus

SCOTT'S BRIDGE OVER GRAND RIVER, PAINESVILLE (Circa 1825)

FRANKLIN HOUSE, PAINESVILLE

From "American Mercury"
Hartford (Conn.)
September 13, 1804

CAPTAIN ABRAHAM SKINNER
Courtesy of Mrs. Sterling Smith

GENERAL EDWARD PAINE
in his later years

FARM RESIDENCE OF THOMAS LLOYD
Originally Lloyd's Tavern, Wickliffe

LIGHTHOUSE AT FAIRPORT — 1825
Built by Jonathan Goldsmith
Courtesy of the Fairport Marine Museum

BLAIR BRIDGE, PERRY-LEROY TWP.
Last covered bridge in Lake County

THE FIRST LAKE COUNTY COURT HOUSE
now the City Hall of Painesville

THE REVEREND JOSEPH BADGER
1757-1846
From *Proceedings of the Grand Lodge of Ohio*

THE REVEREND IRA EDDY
Courtesy of the
Painesville Methodist Church

PAINESVILLE IN 1848
The Methodist Church, the First Church
and the Lake County Court House
Drawn by Henry Howe

Drawn by Henry Howe in 1846.

WILLOUGHBY
Methodist Church, Medical College, Presbyterian Church

Flavius Josephus
Huntington

Stone Schoolhouse, Concord
Built 1841, picture circa 1871

Joseph Smith, Jr.

Mormon Temple

Dr. John H. Mathews home — originally on N. State St., now on
Lake Erie Campus. Built by Jonathan Goldsmith

Dr. Jahial Parmly
*Courtesy of the
University of Pennsylvania*

Harriet Wolcott Beard
Painted by her son,
James H. Beard

Eber Howe
Founder of the
Painesville Telegraph

TRUMBULL MILL
Undershot wheel

THOMPSON'S CHAIR FACTORY, CONCORD
Flume from the dam center — overshot wheel not visible
Courtesy of Mr. Serono Pomeroy

MR. AND MRS. JOHN S. CASEMENT on their wedding trip
Courtesy of Mrs. Harold Furlong

ABEL KIMBALL
Courtesy of Mr. Carl Kimball

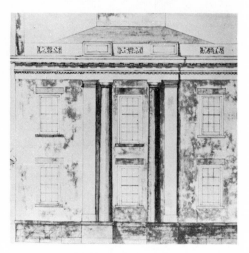

BANK OF GEAUGA
Original drawing
by Jonathan Goldsmith
*Courtesy of the Western
Reserve Historical Society*

THE "ASA CHILDS"
Built on the beach at Mentor Headlands, launched April 22, 1878
Courtesy of Mrs. Lynn Tucker

CLEVELAND, PAINESVILLE AND ASHTABULA R. R. BRIDGE,
GEAUGA FURNACE COMPANY AND ERIE STREET BRIDGE, PAINESVILLE

PRODUCTS OF PEASE MILL, CONCORD

GENERAL JAMES A. GARFIELD (center)
AND HIS STAFF

LAFAYETTE BLAIR

CIVIL WAR ILLUSTRATION
By Frank Beard, son of James

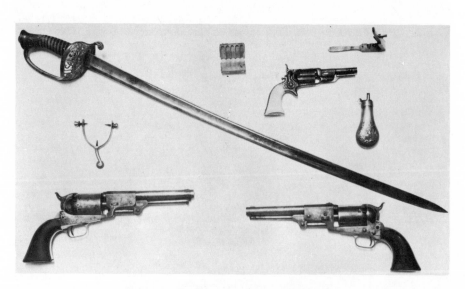

GENERAL GARFIELD'S CIVIL WAR ARMS

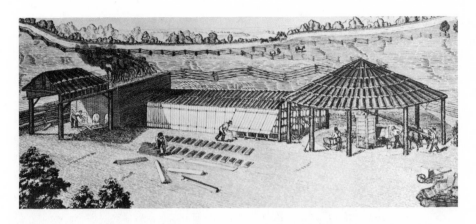

THE PENFIELD BRICK AND TILE PLANT — 1853

Courtesy of Mr. Eugene Kerven

RES. OF L. GREEN, PERRY, LAKE Co. O.

WESTERN RESERVE NURSERY
L. Green, Proprietor, Perry

HOME OF DR. O. S. ST. JOHN, later Andrews School
Corner of Erie and Vine Streets, Willoughby

THOMAS W. HARVEY

AT LAKE ERIE SEMINARY — 1890
May Lockwood Oliver, Annette Fitch
Brewer and Gertrude McClure Dice

INTERURBAN STATION, WILLOUGHBY

THE VULCAN — 1914 ANNOUNCEMENT
From *Treasury of Early American Automobiles*

THE TELEPHONE EXCHANGE
in Mentor, circa 1905

MAIN STREET, PERRY
Circa 1915

DONAHEY'S COMMENTS
ON PAINESVILLE
Circa 1920
Drawn for the
Cleveland Plain Dealer

HAPPY HOOLIGAN
Reprinted from
Ohio Art and Artists

fell, his horse was limping, and they were alone in the deep woods. Eddy dismounted and, clinging to her tail, let the horse sense her way at her own pace. They reached Bainbridge exhausted, long after the meeting was over.

Through piercing cold and devastating heat, often without adequate provisions, Ira Eddy persevered in his good work. His years here brought comfort to many people and to him a personal joy. In 1817 he married Nancy Brigden, a member of his Concord congregation. Although he went on to other places, our communities could feel that the Reverend Eddy was not only a part of their heritage, but that our people, hills and valleys would always be a part of his life.

BAPTIST CHURCHES

Baptist groups are reported to have met as early as 1816 in Madison and at about the same time in Mentor and Perry. However, no missionaries are mentioned in any of the early records. The Baptist Mission Board had not yet taken the field in frontier work. No one seems to have given the small local gatherings a helping hand.

Nonetheless, Baptist Churches were formed. In 1826 Leroy Church was organized, in 1831 Madison reorganized, and in 1836 Perry's Baptist congregation assembled. The same year Thomas Richmond built a church for Baptists in his little town. The building and the congregation, led by the Reverend E. W. Freeman, later moved to Painesville.

AN EPISCOPAL CHURCH

The Episcopal Church had been established by the colonial Royal Governors as a branch of the Church of England. It was not popular with the Puritans as it was from this church that they had fled. However, in Connecticut in 1722, an American Episcopal movement was started by Timothy Cutler, rector of Yale College. His position in the community drew attention to his conversion, and it encouraged an interest which produced a strong church, full of men and women with a deep love for its liturgy.

A parish was organized in Painesville in 1824 by the Reverend Silas C. Freeman. The Episcopal services were first held in the hotel on the Park. Ten years later the Reverend John Hall directed construction of the first church, a clapboard building on the site of the present St. James Church.

THE GREAT REVIVAL

With the coming of some comforts and ease in daily living, the Western Reserve pioneer joined the rest of the country in the flood of religious fervor which swept across the frontier after 1824. It was a time when each man wanted to be saved in exactly the right way and was fearful that his neighbor would not see the light and be among the elect on the great day of judgment. Everyone argued creeds and dogmas. Interest in religion became frenzied; the Great Revival entered the lives of our people.

The Great Revival was the period of camp meetings, when families from miles around would gather to hear a visiting preacher. The meetings lasted several days, with sermons morning, noon and night. Excitement grew as one person after another "got religion," and often gave way to emotional demonstrations such as rolling on the ground, shaking, weeping, laughing, and shouting prayers.

Such a revival meeting was held by the Perry Baptist Church in 1836 and many people were moved to join the faith. So successful was the preaching, in fact, that before they could be baptized, a Methodist asked the Baptist minister to come with his new converts to help the Methodists start a revival. The Baptists agreed, only to find at the end of the meeting that not one of their converts would join the Baptist Church. The Methodists were elated, and reportedly said, "The Baptists shook the tree and we got the birds!"

It is hard to understand the intensity of the interdenominational rivalries of those days. Each church seemed bent on upholding its own ideals and did its best to point out the errors in other beliefs. Even within a single church small groups broke away over some minute point of difference.

CAMPBELL AND HIS DISCIPLES

Alexander Campbell, a popular Revival orator in frontier pulpits, believed that these church arguments worked against the Kingdom of God. He proposed a simple creed, based on the early New Testament church, which he felt offered a solid doctrine for a brotherly union. He called his new group the Disciples of Christ or the Christian Church.

Campbell preached his doctrine widely and effectively throughout the Reserve, and one of his early converts was Sidney Rigdon, pastor of the Mentor Baptist Church. Describing Rigdon in *The Early History of the Disciples in the Western Reserve*, A. S. Hayden said, "Sidney Rigdon was an orator of no inconsiderable abilities. In person he was full medium height, rotund in form; of countenance, while speaking, open and winning, with a little cast of melancholy. His action was graceful, his language copious, fluent in utterance, with articulation clear and musical. Yet he was an enthusiast and unstable. His personal influence with an audience was very great; but many, with talents far inferior, surpassed him in judgment and permanent power with the people. He was just the man for an awakening."

Stirred by Ridgon's eloquence and led by M. S. Clapp, nearly the whole Mentor Church accepted Campbell's doctrine in 1828. A Disciple Church was organized in Perry the following year and grew rapidly with the enthusiasm of the Parmly brothers to support it. In 1830 another congregation assembled on Waite Hill in Chagrin Township. Rigdon made so many converts in Kirtland that a separate group was formed there.

In the days of the Great Revival, Campbell's philosophy of brotherly union did not entirely stop discussion over fine points of belief even in his own churches. The Kirtland Disciples had many questions and grew ready to realign themselves with others of mutual interests. They were to find their answer in Joseph Smith's new Mormon teachings.

Chapter IX

The Saints Among Us

While Sidney Rigdon was preaching to his Disciples of Christ, young Joseph Smith, Jr. was gathering listeners in Palmyra, New York, describing his revelations from God. In these holy visitations, Joseph said he learned of Golden Tablets that had lain buried for fourteen centuries in a mound nearby. Guided by the Angel Moroni, young Smith unearthed the Tablets and found them plates of gold alloy, seven inches wide, eight inches long and bound in a volume, six inches thick. Each plate was said to be "not quite as thick as tin" and each was inscribed with unusual characters and symbols. Smith also found tools to translate the signs, and he undertook the task with utmost secrecy.

MORMONISM

This translated message from the Golden Tablets became the foundation of a new faith, Mormonism, named after the Angel Mormon, father of Moroni. Mormonism was based on the belief that the American Indians were direct descendants of the ancient Hebrews. A Mormon house of worship, as it is with the Hebrews, was called a "Temple," and those who did not accept the Mormon doctrines were called "Gentiles." Mormon followers believed in the second coming of Christ and called themselves the Church of Jesus Christ of Latter-day Saints.

From the first, Smith's family and friends were interested in his revelations from God. When he read the words from the Book of Mormon, many were convinced that God had made Himself known to Smith. Those who accepted the new religion converted others. Soon Mormons went out from New York State to take the new Book's teachings to other areas. That year, 1830, travel was still hazardous and difficult, but this did not discourage the Latter-day Saints.

Four missionaries started westward to take the *Book of Mormon* to the Indians in Missouri. On the way one of the quartet, Parley P. Pratt, suggested they visit his former Baptist Brother, now a Disciple of Christ, Sidney Rigdon of Mentor. Rigdon examined the new religious writings and invited the missionaries to show their Book to the "common-stock people" living in a small colony at Kirtland. In this group of Disciples were eleven families who said they "lived together, shared all things in common in great peace and union." They listened to the Saints with enthusiasm.

Before Parley Pratt and the other missionaries went on to Missouri, they baptized Sidney Rigdon, those of his Mentor church who followed him, and the group in Kirtland. In the Chagrin River one hundred twenty-seven people were baptized and became members of the Mormon Church. The Mormons in this area were now greater in number than the believers in New York State. Deciding to unite the two groups, Prophet Joseph Smith, Jr. led the eastern Saints to Kirtland in January 1831.

A MORMON COLONY IN KIRTLAND

Smith continued to describe his private revelations from God, and it was in this way that he received instructions on matters of policy and how to deal with problems or doubts among his followers. To him, Ohio was only a way station on the road to the real Zion. He revealed to his Saints that their holy city would be created in Missouri. With this in mind he sent out missionaries, two by two, not only to locate and start the perfect colony, but also to preach the Mormon gospel. Some went west, some east and some to Canada. It was here in Kirtland that the Prophet began to show his remarkable powers of organization and leadership.

He introduced an elaborate system of priesthood to which all men belonged, teachers, deacons, priests, elders, bishops, apostles, in successive ranks so that the faithful could climb to influence and responsibility. He strove for an orderly community of brotherly love and on one occasion when his converts became restless under his administration, another revelation lashed at them: "Wo [sic] unto you rich men, that will not give your substance to the poor, for your riches will canker your souls. . . . Wo [sic] unto you poor men, whose hearts are not broken, whose spirits are not contrite, and whose bellies are not satisfied, and whose hands are not stayed from laying hold upon other men's goods, whose eyes are full of greediness, and who will not labor with your own hands! But blessed are the poor who are pure in heart, whose hearts are broken, and whose spirits are contrite, for they shall see the kingdom of God coming in power and great glory unto their deliverance; for the fatness of the earth shall be theirs."

THE TEMPLE IS BUILT

Many Mormons gave up eastern farms and businesses to come to Kirtland and begin anew the struggle for existence, and they found it an effort to glean a bare living. Under physical and financial stress, the Saints were reluctant to begin construction of a great Temple which Prophet Smith desired. (Details of the measurements of the Temple had come to Smith in another revelation from the Lord.) Every male member of the Church was expected to donate one-seventh of his time and finances to the project.

For three years Mormons toiled to build their Temple. Men dragged trees by team from nearby forests. Stone was cut in the Stannard quarry two miles south of Kirtland and at Russell's quarry one mile south. The Prophet himself was the foreman of the stone-cutting operations. Women spun and wove cloth and sold their treasured jewelry to provide funds for supplies. The project began to gain momentum with contagious enthusiasm.

Sidney Rigdon did masonry work on the building, directed by the master-mason, Jacob Bump. Fine china and glassware were crushed into the plaster so that the Temple would sparkle in the sun. Women even sacrificed their long hair to be mixed into a superior quality mortar. Brigham Young, one of the recent converts, worked as a carpenter and supervised interior woodwork.

This was no common frontier meeting house such as the settlers on the Western Reserve had known to this time. It was to be an enduring, imposing and magnificent structure. Many Mormons all over the country sold their property and personal belongings to send money to Kirtland for the Temple. Begun in June 1833, it was finally dedicated on March 27, 1836. Pride in their accomplishment did much to strengthen Mormon unity.

FRICTION BETWEEN SAINTS AND GENTILES

Claims of the Prophet's spectacular healing miracles among his sick followers, with news of strange and wondrous new languages and manifestations from the Lord, brought wagonloads of both converts and curiosity seekers to our Kirtland hills. Soon the Mormon colony numbered three thousand people. This rapid increase alarmed their neighbors.

As long as the Gentile citizens out-numbered the Saints in Kirtland, or in any other Mormon community, all was reasonably peaceful. As increased Mormon immigration threatened the voting power of the community, however, conflict was certain. The Mormons were apt to vote as a solid block and the Gentiles saw that this solidarity might be used to their disadvantage.

Many of the Gentiles also disliked some of the practices of the Mormon religion. Christopher G. Crary, whose life for a decade was tied with the conflicts in Kirtland, wrote in later years, "Their religion is an aggressive one. They [believe they] are the true Saints. The Gentiles are to be destroyed and the end justifies the means." A number of the original pioneers left the community with real fear for their personal safety.

Then, also, there must have been jealousy among the neighboring churches, in that day of strong denominational feeling, to see the Mormon Church grow at such an astounding rate. Whatever the causes, the friction became a serious problem that no revelation was able to solve.

THE PANIC OF 1837

Nor did the Prophet's revelations soften the blow of the nationwide financial Panic of 1837. It took its toll among Mormons and Gentiles alike. A boom in the nation's economy had come to an abrupt halt in July of 1836 when President Jackson tried to stop widespread speculation in government lands and to force local state-chartered banks into more stable financing. These local banks had extended credit in the form of their own currency. Now they were called upon to back up this credit with gold or silver security. Many couldn't and had to close, wiping out much hard-earned savings. Particularly hard hit were people in the western and southern states.

Kirtland's Mormon colony had enjoyed the increased wealth of the boom in the early 1830's along with the rest of the country. Trade began to take the time and attention of the Mormon leaders, and property values in Kirtland soared. Land, which Joseph Smith once purchased for $150 a lot, now cost $500 or a $1,000, depending on location. The Church so prospered in this real estate inflation that the Prophet and his counsellors decided to organize their own bank to handle its financial affairs.

Their request for a charter came at the same moment the Federal government acted to limit the organization of local banks. The Ohio legislature refused to issue a charter for a Mormon bank. Smith then decided that an "anti-banking" company needed no charter, so in November 1836, he formed such an institution. Originally planning to call it "The Kirtland Safety Society Bank," Smith changed the name to read "The Kirtland Safety Society Anti-Banking Company." The name on the currency, engraved before the charter was denied, was altered by type, and the new money was freely circulated. All Mormons were advised to put their entire savings in this new company.

THE SAINTS IN TROUBLE

In the meantime, Smith had gone heavily into debt to keep the colony and Mormonism together. He borrowed wherever he possibly could and accumulated debts, locally and in the east. With their new currency, the Mormons paid off the bigger creditors, but people soon began to wonder about the security behind this paper money.

Word spread that the Mormon bank did not have the resources it claimed. This fear was proved a reality and the Church, and especially its leaders, were in serious difficulty. Not only were the Gentiles aroused, because they had accepted the money in good faith, but the now penniless

Mormons themselves began to shake the foundations of the church. To add to the troubles, creditors filed suits in Geauga courts for recovery of their funds. The entire community was angered, Smith and Rigdon were arrested, imprisoned and fined $1,000 each.

Released from prison, Joseph Smith, Jr. and Sidney Rigdon realized their very lives were in danger. They were being threatened by irate Mormons and furious Gentiles alike. Smith and Rigdon fled from Kirtland in January 1838. Those who remained faithful to their leaders and *The Book of Mormon* migrated to Nauvoo, Illinois, to join the Prophet in establishing another Mormon colony there. Those who renounced the Church stayed in Kirtland or returned to their former homes in the East. As many as seven hundred people left in a single day. Wagons loaded with children, household furnishings and supplies were strung out for miles, moving in slow procession away from their Temple.

MEMORIES OF THE SAINTS

Some of the Smith family remained in Kirtland, however, under the sod of the cemetery. The Prophet's twins were born and died here in April of 1831, just three months after the family arrived. The Smiths had adopted Elder Joseph Murdock's motherless twins, one of whom is also buried in the Temple cemetery. In 1836, Smith's grandmother, Mrs. Asael Smith, died and was laid to rest with the others. Joseph Smith III, son of the Prophet, was born in Kirtland November 6, 1832. He was called "Young Joseph," an affectionate title that was to bring comfort to the hearts of many.

THE RE-ORGANIZED CHURCH OF JESUS CHRIST

After the death of Joseph Smith, Jr. in 1844 at Carthage, Illinois, the Mormon Council of Twelve Apostles elected Brigham Young president and head of their church. He led a courageous band across the plains and mountains to form a colony in Utah. But some of the church members did not believe that Young followed in the footsteps of the Prophet. Many of these scattered in small groups through the middle west. One such group was able to hold together and keep in touch with Young Joseph, who was only twelve at his father's death.

By 1860 Young Joseph had grown to fine manhood. The Reorganized Church of Jesus Christ of Latter Day Saints elected him their president, and new life came into their religion. In 1880 the Ohio courts gave possession of the Kirtland Temple to this Reorganized Church. The judgment was made on the grounds that it represented the true descendants of the original builders in organization, doctrine and practice. All Lake County can rejoice with its members in their "monument to the faith, courage, sacrifice and devotion of the men and women who lived long ago," and take pride with them in their beautiful Temple.

Chapter X

Down by the Old Mill Stream

In the earliest days of settlement on the Western Reserve there was, of course, no factory manufacturing. Still, the pioneers needed fabricated things for both their survival and comfort. Their long arduous trip from the East prevented bringing anything but the most basic tools and equipment. With the very barest essentials a pioneer's cabin became the production center of all those necessary items he could not grow or gather in field or forest. Many things were made with immediate resources and a great deal of ingenuity. The power for this cabin industry was man-woman-child power, lubricated with elbow grease.

FLOUR

A frequent chore in the earliest homes was grinding grain into flour or meal for the family's bread. Some were fortunate to have a quern, a small hand mill, which could reduce wheat to flour. But before the local grist mills were built, most families were dependent on homemade grinders. An oak tree was felled, fire kindled in the stump, in which a large stone slowly burned its way downward, forming a cavity. Into this bowl, when stone and ashes were removed, dried corn was put and pounded with a pestle made of a stone attached with bark to a sapling handle. This corn meal was a staple of the frontier wife's kitchen.

SOAP

Soap-making was another of the important cabin industries. Wood ashes from the hearth were accumulated in the ash hopper, a square funnel built of overlapping boards. On soap-making day, several buckets of water were poured over the ashes making a lye solution which was caught in a trough to fill the family's big iron kettle. Over an outdoor fire the lye was boiled down until it was "strong enough to float an egg," and then allowed to cool. In the meantime a crock of grease had been put near the fire to melt. The grease crock contained bits of left-over fat from daily cooking: bacon rinds, pot skimmings, scraps of suet, all tried out, clarified and strained. This melted grease was added to the lye and stirred vigorously. If the housewife's hand was skilled and the proportions of fat and lye correct, a thick cohesive goo formed. A handful of salt, when that rare substance was available, made the finished product hard enough to cut into cakes. With this homemade cleaner, hard or soft, many a frontier wife washed floors, dishes, clothes and children.

CANDLES

Lighting a cabin at night or on dark days was always a problem. Firelight from the hearth was at first the only illumination. In New England crude oil lamps had been filled with whale oil but here, far from the sea, the pioneers who brought lamps with them had only bear "oil," usually too precious for food or soap to be burned. As time and tallow became available, women made their own candles. Tallow candles were made from the fat of sheep or cattle by a simple, though time-taking process. A row of double-length candle wicks, hung over a stick, were dipped into the iron kettle, now filled with warm tallow. They were hung to dry, dipped again and again until the candle reached the desired size. The process is similar to the way you roll a snowball until enough snow clings to it to make a snowman.

Later, every household was equipped with a candle mold, a rack of metal tubes into which the warm tallow could be poured around the wicks with much less effort. By either method, candle making was a winter job. It came after the fall slaughtering and when the tallow, set away from the hearth, would cool rapidly.

MAPLE SUGAR

With the first thaw of spring, the great iron kettle was put to another use. It was time for sugar making. Hard maples were pegged and buckets were hung to collect the sap. The kettle was put over an outdoor fire, kept going day and night when the sap was running. All the family worked bringing in the buckets, adding wood to the fire, taking off the scum as it formed, and stirring the thickening syrup. This would be the only sweets they would see for the next year, unless someone was lucky enough to find a wild bee tree with its honey. So it was that willing hands were always available for sugar-making.

CLOTHING

Another cabin industry was the preparation of cloth to dress the family. Carded (combed), spun and woven by hand, flax and wool provided the basic material for the pioneers' wardrobe. "Homespun" described an accomplishment as well as a fabric.

The yarn, or sometimes the finished cloth, was also colored at home with the natural dyes found in every cabin clearing. Sumach berries gave a variety of tans, black walnut hulls light to dark brown, and pine needles produced a green. The early spring flower, bloodroot, made a glowing orange and the summer pokeberries could be used for pinks and lavenders.

No patterns were available to guide the dressmaker in her task of cutting garments. At Mentor Marsh Peggy Jordan Parker used a unique method. This resourceful mother simply spread her woven fabric on the floor, laid her offspring down on it, and cut the pattern around the child's body.

By 1813 Mrs. Levi Bartram of Madison was considered an expert weaver and she, like other women and girls on the Reserve, was kept busy making material for clothing and bedding. Even the thread she used for sewing was homespun. She trained her daughters in the skill and sometimes paid the family's property taxes by selling her output.

OTHER CABIN PRODUCTS

During evenings and winter months men worked with leather, making harness and rough moccasins. Jonathan Goldsmith, our famous architect, used his boyhood training to make shoes in exchange for much of the work of clearing his farm. Some clothing was also made from leather.

The art of whittling was highly respected too. Men cut out wooden bowls of all sizes and shapes, pitchforks and "split" brooms. The split broom was made of a small hickory sapling. The splits were stripped up with a jackknife for eight or ten inches. When the heart of the wood was reached, it was too brittle to strip and was cut off. All that was then needed was to smooth the shaft into a comfortable handle. Men's jackknives carved too such simple toys as blocks, tops, boats and dolls to delight their children.

All the while the housewife sat in the evenings she too kept busy sewing, weaving or knitting mittens and caps, sweaters and stockings. Nothing was ever discarded and no time was ever wasted in these early days.

INDUSTRY OUTSIDE THE CABIN

The first industry of the Western Reserve outside the cabin was the grist mill. Here one large grindstone was rotated over another stationary stone. Wheat, poured between them, sifted out as flour. White bread was added to cornmeal pone on our pioneer menus, and the drudgery of home grinding was over.

Power for the early mills varied. In Harpersfield animals were used to turn the grindstone. Madison's Abel Kimball operated a wind-driven wheel. Most popular of all was water power, a familiar idea brought overseas by the Pilgrims.

By the early nineteenth century two types of waterwheels were in use. More efficient, the overshot wheel was built at a natural waterfall or a dam where both the force of the water's current and the weight of the water falling on the wheel would turn the shaft. The undershot wheel, built level with the stream, had only the water's force to turn it. Both wheels depended on a sufficient flow of water and could not easily operate in dry seasons. Our early mills used both types of wheels.

WATER-POWERED MILLS

David Abbott's mill, the first on the Reserve, was built on the Chagrin River in 1798. Spencer Phelps, driving his yoke of oxen, had dragged his grain-laden sled through the woods from Leroy Township to the Humphrey mill, built in 1801 at Austinburg, the first mill in Ashtabula County. In 1803 Eleazer Paine hired Isaac and James Thompson to build a mill at the mouth of Tiber Creek below New Market.

Other grist mills were built along the rivers and streams until nearly every corner of the county had access to one. Among these were Jordan's mill in Concord Township, Trumbull's in south Madison on Grand River and Eli Bond's in Perry. James Ford built his grist mill on Arcola Creek in north Madison, William Judd built on the Chagrin River at the main ford in 1804, John Walcott and William Webster built further south. Even little Marsh Creek on Hopkins Road in Mentor was harnessed to provide power for Joseph Sawyer's mill. Joel Scott operated a mill at Champion in 1808, about the same time that David French built on Kellogg Creek in Concord. This partial list shows the service these grist mills gave our pioneer families.

SAW MILLS

Our settler's log cabins were sound and sturdy structures but they were uncomfortable and drafty. Wind, rain and snow had a way of sifting through the cracks. Also, logs were far more clumsy to handle than boards but, most of all, the pioneers wanted the finished clapboard houses they had known in the east.

Many of our early water-powered saw mills were near grist mills or combined both operations, such as Abbott's or Wolcott and Webster's.

By 1816 Benjamin Bates built a saw-grist mill in Leroy Township, and two years later Hendrick Paine built his mill in Paine's Hollow. Holmes and Card had a saw-grist mill in Kirtland, as did Williams in Concord.

DISTILLERIES

Every community soon had its distillery to turn surplus grain into whiskey. This was a usable product which could be both stored and transported much more conveniently than the grain. Whiskey was commonly used as a medium of exchange in the early days. Even school teachers and ministers received part of their pay in a jug of whiskey, and all the neighbors, gathered for a barnraising or harvest, expected a generous supply to cheer their efforts. While some stories of excessive drinking have come down to us, by and large, the tremendously hard labors of the pioneers counteracted any ill effects of the alcohol.

BLACKSMITHS

All of the early industries, cabin or mill, needed the services of the blacksmith. Not only did he make shoes for the oxen and horses, but he also sharpened scythes, mended plows, made chains for heavy hauling, and hand-forged hardware for harnesses, wagons and parts for the mills.

In the center of the smithy was a high hearth with an everburning fire. A huge bellows at the side, blowing in a draft under the grate, made the intense heat necessary to turn the iron malleable. The anvil stood nearby on a heavy oak stump. In one corner a canvas hammock hung from ropes and pulleys, used to lift oxen who never learn, as does a horse, to raise their hooves. The smith, in his heavy leather apron, swung his sledge with even strokes to pound and shape the necessary tools for the pioneer communities.

Ebenezer Smith, you will remember, was the blacksmith who made the tools to cut the Reserve's first mill stones for David Abbott. Unionville welcomed its first blacksmith in 1805, and Jabez Smith set up his forge in Leroy Township. By 1818 the blacksmith at Paine's Hollow served the pioneers as well as the needs of that growing industrial community.

TANNERIES

The tannery was another enterprise which freed men from much work. Tanning was a highly specialized art and although the tools were simple, success depended on knowledge of special formulas for solutions in which the hides were treated. The main ingredient was tannin, ground from oak or hemlock bark.

Every tanner had a large vat for soaking the undressed hides. A water wheel provided the power to scour and roll them and the stream was used for rinsing the treated leather. Although the whole process of professional curing of hides might take as long as a year, the product was of considerably higher quality than the output of most cabins.

As early as 1803 Meigs S. Brown built a tannery at New Market. Samuel Holmes operated the first tannery at Champion in 1806 and Richard Woolsey finished leather for the Chagrin settlers after 1816.

WOOLEN MILLS

Shearing sheep was man's work, but making the wool into clothing was done by the women. Woolen mills gave women the relief from drudgery that the tanneries had the men. The early mills, like that of Howe and Rogers on Big Creek in Concord, did not attempt to do spinning or weaving, but they did the first steps of washing and carding the wool. Then the woven product of the hand looms could be returned to the mill for fulling and napping, which turned the housewife's rough fabric to smooth, firm, lustrous material.

Later woolen mills, such as Dodd's, had powered weaving looms. John Augustus Dodd was a trained woolen worker from Leeds, England, who accepted a job at the Wolcott-Wheelock Mill in Pleasant Valley, Willoughby Township, in 1844. Dodd eventually owned the business and, with his sons, manufactured "Woolen Goods, Cloths, Cassimeres, Sheeting, Flannels, Tweeds, Stocking Yarns, etc." until the turn of the century.

POTASH AND PEPPERMINT OIL

One purely frontier industry was the ashery, such as the one in Paine's Hollow, Leroy. Here men used water, ashes of hard woods, and a simple device to produce potash. It was made by reducing the ashes and water with intense heat and evaporation to a strong alkaline substance. Making potash was an important frontier industry because the product, much in demand in the east, was light weight and easy to transport. It was used in wool manufacturing to clean the wool before spinning and again as the wool was dyed. Used also in glass making, soap making and in the preparation of medicines, potash was for many years one of the major exports from this region to the east on the Erie Canal.

Another frontier product which brought good money for its weight was peppermint oil. Oil of peppermint was not just a candy flavoring. In those early days it was considered a useful herb for medicine, so it became an important cash crop. Sites of two peppermint stills have been located in Mentor Township, one on the Reynolds farm in the southeast corner, and another on the Mather farm on Jackson Street near Hopkins

Road. There were undoubtedly many more in the county, judging by the amount of peppermint oil exported from Fairport in 1847. (See chart at the end of this chapter.)

IRON MAKING

Much of our early industry would not have grown without iron products. Local deposits of bog iron were discovered in shallow pockets along the north ridge in Madison and Perry, and along the south ridge in Madison, Leroy, Concord and Mentor. This spongy limonite ore, although it contained little more than 25% pure iron, was still suitable for foundry work. Other ore hauled to the Reserve by ox team cost a forbidding 25c a pound, but the local ore was an economical 6c a pound.

Charcoal was also used in the manufacture of iron. Between harvest and spring planting, local farmers earned 37½c for every cord of wood cut from our abundant forests and hauled to the charcoal kilns. At the kilns, skilled colliers stacked the logs in a pit carefully so as to allow some ventilation. The mound, covered with sod until it resembled a huge beehive, was then ignited. When the wood at the bottom was burning well the vents were closed and the mass of timber slowly simmered, converting itself into charcoal. After the kiln cooled, the charcoal was stored in sheds until needed as fuel for the furnace.

BLAST FURNACES

An early blast furnace was crude but very sturdily built of brick and stone. It had a stack usually thirty-two feet high, twenty-one feet square at the base and tapering to eleven feet square at the top. The furnace sat at the foot of a hillside and was loaded at the top by means of a bridge from the bank.

Layers of ore, charcoal and limestone, the fluxing agent, were dumped into the stack and, as the charge settled, more layers were added. Air, to increase the burning, was forced in by simple blowing machines driven by water power. Once or twice each day the waste, or slag, was drawn off and the plug broken. Molten iron rushed from the furnace into troughs to form sow bars (pig iron) or was poured into molds to produce the desired shape of cast iron.

These early furnaces were a seven day a week operation where men worked hauling in raw materials (about 3 tons of ore, 1½ tons of limestone and 265 bushels of charcoal were needed to make one ton of pig iron) while other men took turns minding the kilns and furnaces around the clock. At peak operation thirty-five tons of iron could be produced in a week. The furnaces gave employment to many of our residents, furnished cheap iron products to our households and farms, and brought new money into the area through their exports.

IRON WORKS

Probably the first furnace built in what is now Lake County was that of Hart and Newell in Mentor Township. Here were manufactured cast iron plows, the first made on the Reserve, and cast iron bells shipped to a Connecticut clock company.

In 1824 the Geauga Furnace was founded at Pepoon's Crossing (now Route No. 20) on Grand River. This company made kettles and later turned out cooking stoves and fancy parlor stoves. Changing management and name several times, this furnace continued in operation until about 1870, longest lived of any of our iron industry.

The year 1825 saw the beginning of three more furnaces: the Incorporate Company in Concord, probably the one owned by Eliakim Field who encouraged our Manx settlement; Thorndike and Drury's in Perry, later called the Railroad Furnace and Root and Wheeler's Erie Furnace in Madison (now Arcola Creek and Route No. 20). In 1832 the Clyde Company was formed in Madison and built a furnace (which may have been our first hot blast type) just over the county line in Ashtabula County. Furnaces were also built in Paine's Hollow and in Cascade Hollow. T. H. Rust built near the Incorporate Company and made stoves which were described as "very heavy cast iron throughout about ¾ of an inch thick, a type all their own, round, about 5 feet in diameter with an elevated oven."

ARCOLE FURNACE

In 1828 Samuel Wilkeson of Buffalo, New York, and Uri Seeley of Painesville purchased the Erie Furnace, renamed it after Wilkeson's Buffalo firm, "Arcole," and incorporated the company with a capital stock of $100,000. Seeley was a prosperous farmer, widely known for his energy, integrity and activity in community affairs.

Wilkeson had become familiar in the area as a Pittsburgh salt merchant, carrying on trade as far as Lake Erie. During the War of 1812 he built a fleet of boats at Fairport for General William Henry Harrison. With the opening of the Erie Canal he had gone into canal boating and soon developed a burning determination to make Buffalo the leading port on Lake Erie. He was interested in Arcole Furnace because it would serve as a means to stimulate shipping of much needed manufactured goods in and out of Buffalo. The citizens of that town recognized their obligation to him and his gravestone reads, "He built the city by building its harbor."

As long as the supply of local bog iron lasted, Arcole was the most prosperous of our furnaces. In 1839, it exported 1400 tons of pig iron, said to be of excellent quality. It produced stoves, hollow ware and potash kettles. For nearly two decades it was the center of a busy, flourishing community. Wilkeson's enterprise did not leave as permanent a mark on our community as it did on Buffalo, but he and Seeley added considerable wealth and vigor to our industrial life.

SHIPBUILDING

Because of the needs for transportation on the Lake, shipbuilding early became an important industry. David Abbott had built his schooner, the *Cuyahoga Packet,* on the Chagrin River in 1805, and she sailed the Lake until captured by the British in the War of 1812. Joel Scott, who had bridged the river at New Market, had a shipyard in the Painesville Flats and supervised construction of two schooners that saw service on the Lake. The first ship, the *Champion,* was launched in 1813. The other, the *Farmer,* commanded by Captain J. K. Whaley, sailed down the river in the high water of 1820, with young Harry Babcock as cabin boy. He recalled: "As the schooner rounded the point at Skinner's Landing, old General Paine danced down to the river bank and threw a jug of whiskey to the crew to express his compliments to the new craft."

Richmond and Fairport also had shipbuilders, and craft of various sizes were constructed on the beach at both Mentor Headlands and Perry. Ellensburgh, at the mouth of Arcola Creek in Madison Township, probably produced more ships than any other site. In 1825, the year the Erie Canal opened, a steamboat was built there by a man named Fuller. He was something of a mechanical genius and built the entire craft himself. He shaped the timbers, forged the spikes and necessary engine parts. The cylinder for the engine was made of wood heavily banded with iron. Fuller's was the first steamboat built west of Buffalo and the third such ship on Lake Erie.

Ellensburgh was an active harbor for many years. The long dock built out into the Lake was used by ships importing limestone from Kelley's Island for Arcole Furnace, and more ships sailed to Buffalo with Arcole products. The shipbuilding yards of Erastus and Edmund Lockwood were in brisk competition with those of Harlow and Alanson Bailey. Two or three masted schooners, single-deck shallow cargo vessels, were launched parallel to the beach and sailed past the dock and three government beacon lights into the open lake. Sails for many of these ships were expertly sewn in the cabinet shop of Joel T. Norton, where other furnishings for ships were also made.

As one enterprise attracted another some areas in the county soon became industrial centers. The housewife came to rely on the grist and woolen mills as the mills themselves began to rely on others for products they needed. Such concentrations of industry developed in areas other than Ellensburgh. Paine's Hollow in Leroy supplied many goods for farmer and housewife alike. A very busy center was Cascade Hollow in Concord.

MORE MILLS ARE BUILT

Turning mills and cabinet shops brought many luxuries and comforts to our citizens. Daniel Able turned handles for axes, hoes and plows on his water powered lathe in Paine's Hollow. Products from Thompson's chair factory on Jordan Creek in Concord and the Newell factory in Kirtland offered to replace the crude furniture of the pioneers. Hand-whittled necessities were now disappearing with the introduction of the turning lathe.

Isaac Bedient operated the first woodenware factory in Cascade Hollow, Concord. He turned out wooden bowls and sugar kegs, spool boxes and "knickknacks." While he ran the lathe, his wife walked to neighboring communities peddling their wares. In the 1840's David Mills Pease, a trained craftsman, came to Cascade Hollow. He converted a sawmill into a factory and began turning out fancy spice boxes, dainty spool holders, candle sticks and button boxes. Succeeded by his sons and grandsons, the Pease Mill operated for over half a century.

As roads improved, wagon shops were built. Willoughby had a prosperous business, Paine's Hollow had another, as did the village of Kirtland. On Jordan Creek was a button factory and near it was the Norton Clock Works. Although agricultural products took the leading role, this 1847 list of exports from Fairport (printed in William Brothers' *Geauga and Lake Counties*) shows something of the value of our local industries. It does not, of course, include exports from Ellensburgh or by ox team.

Ashes [for potash]	$ 25,261
Furniture	10,440
Iron, manufactured	13,649
Iron, pig metal	22,350
Leather	3,883
Lumber, sawed	9,144
Lumber, staves for barrels	9,872
Oil of Peppermint	30,678
Plows	1,043
Wagons	7,800
Miscellaneous articles	22,190
Agricultural products	305,718
Total	$462,028

It is not difficult to imagine how the growth of industry improved pioneer life. With better tools, a man had greater ease in farming. Log cabins were replaced with frame houses and fitted with comfortable furniture. Clothes too took on a more attractive appearance. Buckskin and homespun gave way to finished fabrics. The water-powered mills and furnaces made available the equipment and the comforts our settlers had known in the east. The wilderness had in truth retreated.

Further progress in the economic and cultural life of our society would depend upon the development of a sound banking system and more improvements in transportation. The growing population of farmers, manufacturers and merchants needed both a stable financial climate and an efficient means of moving goods to the markets within and beyond Lake County's borders.

Chapter XI

An Expanding World

Currency had been a problem from the earliest days of our Republic. The Continental Congress was not given the power to levy taxes and had been forced to issue paper money to carry on the Revolutionary War. The old phrase, "Not worth a continental," is the literal history of that first scrip. Peace and the Constitution did not bring an immediate solution. In 1791 a national bank was created by Congress. Its notes were honored at full value and it brought stability into the financial picture. When its charter expired in 1811, a swarm of state-licensed banks sprang up, many issuing paper notes without restraint. We have already seen in the case of the Mormon banking experiment, how false security can bring financial ruin to trusting depositors. It is equally true that the development of resources and the interchange of commodities need an adequate supply of some means of exchange. Paper money, good, bad and indifferent, filled a vacuum for commerce.

THE STOREKEEPER'S BOOKKEEPING

Jonathan Card served as an apprentice in a Painesville store in the early 1830's. His *Autobiography* describes the credit system used: "Our sales were almost entirely on credit of a year's time, mainly to farmers all through Geauga and part of Ashtabula County (Lake County not being then organized). The rule to a considerable extent with the farmer was to pay after being sued. . . . I do not remember an instance of the sale of property, money would always come. . . . But I do remember a number of . . . families [who were being sued] trading right along as usual."

A simple swap or barter method continued to be popular for a good many years. An 1840 advertisement declared: "The subscriber would respectfully inform the inhabitants of Painesville and vicinity that he has opened a Store on the corner of Main and St. Clair, where he offers for sale, at prices to suit the times, all kinds of HATS and CAPS adapted to the season. All kinds of produce received in payment, Cash not refused."

Cash itself was another problem for the merchant. It has been estimated that at this time there were over 1600 varieties of notes in circulation. A storekeeper's profits depended upon his astuteness in giving a premium for good money, discounting correctly indifferent money and refusing the bogus. George B. Pease, who sold hardware at the sign of the Padlock, was advertising in 1840: "MONEY WANTED. I want $5000 dollars in Eastern funds for which I will pay a fair premium if presented in fifteen days." Judging by another notice in the same paper, his new shipment of shovels, spades, forks, nails and rope, "JUST RE-CEIVED Per Schooner *Ralph Granger,* and for sale very low for Cash," had a wholesaler waiting for payment.

THE BANK OF GEAUGA

The Bank of Geauga was the first local step toward a sound economy. Warren's Western Reserve Bank, chartered in 1812, and Cleveland's Commercial Bank of Lake Erie, opened in 1816, had helped to relieve our financial problems. Our communities welcomed their new bank which was started in Painesville in 1831, the third on the Reserve. The Bank of Geauga, directed by honest and able men, withstood Nineteenth Century's booms and panics, never refusing any demand for payment of specie in exchange for its notes. After the passage of the National Bank Act of 1863, it became the Painesville National Bank. In 1946 it was absorbed by the Cleveland Trust Company.

TRANSPORTATION PROBLEMS

The need for improved transportation has been pressing at every period of United States history. The new Lake County of the 1840's was no exception in this national pattern. While our towns grew and lake traffic was flourishing, transportation to the inland communities was still a problem. The Cleveland-Buffalo road, as we know, followed a natural gravel ridge. Like others, it was dusty in the summer and bumpy all year, but it was at least passable in the spring and fall rains. This was not always so of the roads north and south of the ridges. "Get the farmer out of the mud" was the universal cry.

In the decade after 1840 two methods of improving roads were introduced in this country. The theories of a Scotsman, John Loudon MacAdam, had been proved successful in England and France and gained popularity in the United States. His plan of construction depended on good drainage for the road bed. He built a road of crushed stone, raising the road bed above the land on either side. The thick layer of stone was well rounded to encourage drainage, and good ditches were made at either edge to carry off storm water. Here in Lake County macadam roads were built of local gravel and, gradually, we began to conquer the mud.

PLANK ROADS

The other method, which helped transportation on the Reserve for several years, was the plank road. In 1849 some of the progressive people in Leroy and Concord Townships organized the Lake and Trumbull Plank Road Company. The proposed road from Trumbull Township, Ashtabula County, followed what is now Route 166 across Thompson to meet present Route 86 and continued northwest to Painesville. It was made by laying heavy foundation timbers parallel with the roadway and covering them with wooden planks laid crosswise. Property owners sold right-of-way and timber in exchange for stock in the company. Toll houses were set up at Bostwick's Corners, Weed's Corners and at the edge of Painesville. Typical tolls per mile were: two horse team, 2c; horse and rig, 1½c; saddle horse, 1c; driven cattle, ½c each.

For a decade this road gave the farmers of Concord and Leroy Townships, as well as Thompson and Trumbull, good access to the markets at Painesville and the docks at Fairport. However, the lumber, buried in the mud and exposed to sun, rain and frost, heavy wheels and horses hooves, began to rot away. Before long the uneven surface of Plank Road became almost as unpleasant as the mud and dust. At the end of the Civil War the toll houses closed. With the introduction of road machinery macadam roads could be made better and cheaper.

THE COMING OF THE RAILROADS

Even before the canals opened up transportation to New York and New Orleans, local men began talking about railroads. Ships were serviceable but slow, and the frozen Lake halted traffic for months in the winter. Our merchants needed dependable connections with eastern markets and the steadily growing western ones. Imaginative men looked ahead and predicted a time when trains would hurtle across Ohio, to and through Lake County, at a speed of fifteen miles an hour! Practical men, however, saw the difficulties of financing, obtaining a charter and right-of-way. They understood the challenge of construction at a time when there was little experience to guide them.

THE PAINESVILLE AND FAIRPORT RAILROAD

A group of our citizens was both imaginative and practical. They saw Cleveland growing rapidly as Lake terminal of the Ohio Canal. With a railroad to its door, Fairport would be in an equally promising position. Ralph Granger, James H. Paine, Lemuel G. Storrs, Henry Phelps, Homer Higley, David Hull, Reuben Hitchcock, Peleg P. Sanford, John H. Mathews, Hezekiah King, Solon Corning, Addison Hills, Milo Harris,

Grandison Newell and Jonathan F. Card were the men who obtained a charter in 1835 for the Painesville & Fairport Railroad.

They and their fellow citizens subscribed $19,755 toward the venture, and a loan of $6,182 was obtained from the state. Jonathan Goldsmith agreed to supervise the construction of oak rails and their covering of long thin straps of iron. In 1837 the tracks were opened from the harbor to Painesville, the second railroad in operation in Ohio. With their first equipment consisting of one wooden passenger car and one crude freight car drawn by two horses, the management looked forward confidently to a steam engine. In the meantime they planned to extend the line south to Wellsville on the Ohio River.

These years were a difficult time to be starting a new enterprise. The year 1837 saw the beginning of one of the country's most severe depressions. People had no money to ride a railroad, and there was no market to which to send freight. In 1841 the high water of a spring freshet carried away the bridge near Skinner's Landing. The Company, having exhausted its resources on the first construction, could not rebuild. The Painesville and Fairport Railroad stopped running, and the right-of-way gradually covered with weeds.

THE OHIO RAILROAD

Another local effort to improve transportation was the Ohio Railroad, which had its birth at the Mansion House in Painesville on April 25, 1836. Twelve visionary men from Geauga and Cuyahoga Counties believed they could avoid the heavy expense of grading a railroad bed by placing the track on two rows of piles. They planned a line across the state east from Toledo to Richmond City.

The ease with which the company obtained promises of nearly two million dollars indicates the spirit of the times. People were so eager for good transportation that they were willing to gamble on any mad scheme that might move them out of the mud. A pile driver started to pound down poles in a field near Fremont. A circular saw followed, leveling them. Fifteen miles of stilts stuck up out of the ground when Thomas Richmond began to quarrel with some of the men active in the operation. The other stockholders found he had good reasons for disapproving of his opponents' business methods. The Ohio Railroad was declared bankrupt and many people in the Reserve lost heavily from their investment in it.

It was also the final blow for Thomas Richmond, and the end of his hopes for his little town. He quite literally tore up the village, moving houses to Painesville, shipping some on barges as far west as Milwaukee, burning and tearing down others. Richmond City, like New Market, turned into pastureland.

THE CLEVELAND, PAINESVILLE & ASHTABULA RAILROAD

For nearly ten years no further move was made to bring rail transportation into the county. Then, as construction of the Cleveland, Columbus & Cincinnati line began pushing north, Judge W. W. Branch and Abel Kimball, both of Madison, started talking of building a railroad along the Lake to meet it. Largely through Kimball's efforts in the Ohio Legislature, a charter was obtained in 1848 for the Cleveland, Painesville & Ashtabula Railroad. Supporting the need for such a line, a preliminary survey found that 75,000 hogs and 20,000 head of cattle had been driven through Lake County to Buffalo during the previous season. This would be substantial business for the new railroad, and an organization was formed to interest investors.

Alvin F. Harlow in *The Road of the Century* writes: "Stock subscriptions were badly needed, and Judge Branch toured the Lake shore as a missionary, organizing meetings in every town. He was not a wealthy man; he could buy only one share of the stock for his own, but he atoned for his poverty by his fanatical zeal, maintained against much disbelief and discouragement. Many considered it the height of folly to suppose that a railroad could compete with the Lake steamers between Buffalo and Cleveland. When Branch, in rebuttal, transported by his ardor, soared to the height of predicting the Pacific road and the products of China coming eastward over the C. P. & A., he was greeted by derision, some city editors even delicately alluding to him as a lunatic. But he did win support."

Judge Branch and the other supporters of the Cleveland, Painesville & Ashtabula had more than eloquence working in their favor. Travel on Lake Erie was hazardous as well as slow. Storms come up quickly on our shallow Lake, and rough waters develop very rapidly. Over the years many boats have capsized, but an even worse danger to the early wooden ships was fire. On June 17, 1850, one of the most tragic disasters of the Great Lakes occurred off Willoughby Township's shoreline (just opposite today's Shoregate Shopping Center).

THE *GRIFFITH* DISASTER

The sidewheeler *G. P. Griffith,* out of Buffalo with a full crew, was bound for Sandusky with three hundred passengers. Many were in family groups. Nearly fifty were from Gloucester and Ely, England. More than one hundred were emigrating from Baden, Germany, and there was a small group from Ireland. Off Fairport at 3 A. M. fire was discovered in the cargo hold.

Setting up hand pumps immediately, the crew worked feverishly to extinguish the blaze. Not at first alerted, the passengers awakened with the noise as the fire gained steadily. Some in their nightclothes, some half dressed, they poured out on deck. The Captain, giving up hope of saving his ship, ordered her headed for shore, only to have the vessel strike a sandbar some five hundred feet from land. The *Griffith* swung around abruptly with a jolt, and flames burst out in the forward and after cabins and in the pilot house. The passengers became panic stricken.

Small boats all along the shore hurried to rescue passengers and crew. At sunset that day the full extent of the tragedy became known. Only forty people survived, one hundred and forty were dead and another hundred and twenty were missing. A little cemetery stood on the Lake shore for many years as mute testimony of the accident. But it, like so much of our shoreline, has washed away, and the once recovered bodies have joined those others lost in June 1850.

THE LAKE SHORE ROAD IS BUILT

So fear of lake disasters was added to the reasons for interest in rail service. The Cleveland, Painesville & Ashtabula raised enough cash to sign a contract in 1850 with a firm experienced in building railroads. They pushed the track through rapidly, and the solid iron rails reached Painesville, November 19, 1851. The following day a large delegation of Cleveland people traveled out in two fine cars for the grand opening of what had already become popularly known as "The Lake Shore Road." Met by a procession of Painesville citizens and a brass band, the distinguished guests were greeted by Mayor Palmer, and the Mayor of Cleveland responded. It was a stormy day of rain and snow, but the entire group went to the Courthouse to hear more speeches and to enjoy dinner at the Stockwell House on the east side of the Park. The *Telegraph* account ends: "The train was rather slow in returning to Cleveland, because of the backward motion of the locomobile, there being as yet no apparatus for reversing its position."

JACK CASEMENT COMES TO PAINESVILLE

As work on the railroad continued east, a second crew came in to improve the first rapid construction, to ballast the track, to fill in many small ravines first crossed by trestle work and to lay a second track. In charge of this group was John Stephen Casement, destined to be one of our outstanding citizens.

Casement had been born in New York State in 1829 of parents newly come from the Isle of Man. He had started work as a mere child to help support his family, first as a water-boy with a railroad gang, later as a line walker spiking to the heavy wooden runners the strap iron which served as rails. At sixteen, after the family had moved to Michigan, he continued his railroad career as a laborer on the construction of the Michigan Central. Although short of stature and light weight, he was noted for his strength, energy and endurance. In the spring of 1850, at the age of twenty-one, he came to Ohio and began laying track for the Cleveland, Columbus & Cincinnati, rising to be foreman of a construction gang. In 1853 he signed his first contract on his own. This was to improve the roadbed of the Lake Shore Road.

While he was working on this job, Jack Casement married Frances Jennings of Painesville, and it was here he established his permanent home. But he was not to remain at home for long. His skill as a builder and his ability as a leader of men were eagerly sought in the railroad-hungry era. After earning the rank of General in the Civil War, he and his brother Daniel took the contract for laying track on the eastern half of the Union Pacific project. The construction of this first transcontinental line, crossing the Great Plains and scaling the Rockies, through country infested with hostile Indians, contributed a glamorous chapter in the history of our nation. Casement's spectacular part in the enterprise, including the laying of over eight miles of track in a single day, brought him fame, fortune and a continuing number of railroad contracts.

Painesville, however, did remain his home. He and his family were prominent citizens of the town, always active in its affairs. His vigorous personality left an imprint on our county, as did Mrs. Casement's charm and strong interest in women's rights.

THE IRISH ARRIVE

As the Erie Canal had brought our first Manx settlers, so the railroad brought the Irish. They had begun coming to the United States early in the 19th century seeking freedom to worship as they chose and freedom to have their own political views. Canal and then railroad construction offered them jobs, and immigration was spurred on by serious over-population and poverty in their country.

Some three thousand Irish had helped build the Erie Canal. Many of them moved west to work on the Ohio Canal and a few of these stopped off in Painesville. However, our main Irish immigration began with the arrival of the Lake Shore Road. Working on our farms or on the railroad, they were buoyant and warm hearted, with common sense and a fund of ready wit. They made a place for themselves and were soon absorbed into the community.

SAINT MARY'S CHURCH

The early history of the Irish in Lake County is the history of our first Roman Catholic Church. In the 1840's a priest came out from Cleveland three or four times a year to say mass in the homes of Patrick McGarey, Cornelius Mahoney and Patrick Shelby of Painesville. By 1850 the group had grown large enough so that a young Frenchman, the Reverend Peter Peudeprat, was put in charge of a parish which included Lake, Geauga and Ashtabula Counties. His itinerary was like that of Badger and Eddy. The roads had improved, there were few wild animals, but the area was large, transportation difficult, weather unpredictable. Like the early Protestant missionaries, his life was far from easy.

In his two years here, besides ministering to scattered families, Father Peudeprat established the parish and organized a church in an old frame carpenter shop on South State Street at the end of Washington Street. Father Charles Coquerelle followed him to see the parish grow and flourish. Under his guidance a church was built where the present building stands, and St. Mary's School was established. In 1859 Father Coquerelle listed his flock in Painesville, Perry and Mentor as 135 families, 28 single men (mostly working on the railroad), and 43 single girls. Willoughby had 13 families, 60 souls in all. Wickliffe had 18 families, 72 in all, and Madison had three families. Another religion was firmly established in our county.

DAN BEARD AND PAINESVILLE

While our people were taking part in the development of Lake County and the nation, they were also providing a quiet countryside to inspire one of United States' future leaders. James H. Beard brought his family back to Painesville for a few years in the 1850's. Here, his son Dan found the inspiration out of which grew the Boy Scouts of America. He tells his story in his autobiography, *Hardly a Man is Now Alive.*

"Painesville was nothing less than heaven to me. It was my first experience with trees, fields, flower gardens, a barn, a chicken coop, a cow shed, chickens and a cow. A big wide swinging gate with square flat topped gate posts furnished an entrance to the lane leading to the barn. A glistening white picket fence protected the front yard from the sandy road. . . . In addition to many things I had seldom seen in the city were butterflies, robins, jay birds, purple martins, swallows, passenger pigeons and red headed woodpeckers. . . . The love of all these things was intensified by my child life in Painesville, Ohio. It is difficult for me to convey to the reader an idea of how happy I was when in wading through a field of grain I unexpectedly came upon a meadow lark's nest on the

ground. . . . Painesville, that wonderland where they made their own tobacco pipes, their own matches by dipping pine slivers in melted sulphur,
and where we made our own soap, molded our own candles, raised our
own vegetables and flowers and grew our own pumpkins. I fancy that
I can now and then catch a whiff of the matchless scent of Mother's rose
garden. . . . Everything was wonderful to the little city child, and intense-
ly interesting. The days were all too short."

This love of nature and a self-sufficient life stayed with Dan Beard,
and led him to hunt a way to open up such experiences for other boys.
A heritage from Lake County spreads across our great nation at every
Boy Scout meeting.

Chapter XII

We Meet the Nation's Crisis

While iron rails were stretching across our country, in the North a very different kind of railroad was also growing: the Underground Railroad. This was not really underground nor did it have iron rails. It was organized by people who wanted to help runaway slaves reach freedom in Canada.

As early as 1812 an abolition society had been formed in Ohio by men who believed in human freedom for everyone and who wanted slavery abolished. Some members of these societies, "conductors" on the Underground Railroad, fed and clothed slaves as they arrived at their doors, and passed them on to the next "station." Under cover of darkness they sent them with a guide on foot or horseback or concealed in a wagon under produce or bags of grain. "Station" keepers had to be shrewd, secretive and courageous. When slave catchers were reported in the neighborhood, the runaways were hidden in secret rooms, haystacks or swamps until danger of capture passed.

UNDERGROUND RAILROAD ROUTES

Several Underground routes from the South converged at Concord. One came from Akron, Hudson and Chagrin Falls, another directly north from Ravenna. From Warren a "road" ran through Parkman and Chardon, another by way of Mesopotamia. Still another came through Bloomfield, Hartsgrove and Montville. A line of stations also ran from Warren into Madison Township.

In Concord Eber Howe kept wayfarers at "Nigger Hollow," along what is now Fay Road. As many as one hundred slaves were gathered at one time in Seth Marshall's barn on Painesville's river bank. They were sent downstream to Fairport, or whisked across the river to C. C. Jennings' or Uri Seeley's to be out of the way of inquiring agents. Slave catchers were sometimes outwitted when their intended victims were hustled to shelter in Madison, or on to Jefferson. But usually the

Negroes went to Fairport where Phineas Root hid them in his harbor warehouse until they could be smuggled aboard ship for Canada. Even Samuel Butler, though keeper of the Government lighthouse, hid men in the attic of his tavern.

In Madison there were prominent names among the Abolitionists, men like Kimball, Merriman and Winchester. Unionville Tavern still has evidence of its Underground station from which the fugitives were sent to the docks at Ellensburgh whenever a friendly captain was willing to take a load across the Lake to freedom.

ANTI-SLAVERY FEELING GROWS

Since 1832 President Storrs and the faculty of Western Reserve College at Hudson had been preaching and lecturing against slavery. These sermons and lectures were the real beginning of anti-slavery propaganda in northern Ohio. By 1838 the Reserve had a more definite anti-slavery character than any other territory of similar size in the United States. With the exception of Willoughby which was more conservative, our communities shared this anti-slavery feeling with the rest of the Reserve.

One exciting incident showed the high pitch of local feeling. In August 1843, two Kentucky slaves, Milton and Lewis Clarke, spoke to an enthusiastic audience in what is now the Madison Post Office. The following day Milton was captured and beaten by four slave catchers. Before he could be taken away, men from Madison, Painesville and Unionville united to stop them. Charging the slave catchers with assault, the Lake Countians had time to arrange Clarke's escape before the case could be brought to trial. Ardent local abolitionists kept their vow that "no slaves shall be captured in Lake County." The Clarkes continued lecturing in the North against slavery, and Lewis, who met Harriet Beecher Stowe, was later recreated as her character George Harris in *Uncle Tom's Cabin.*

Many Negroes must have remembered the good care they received in Lake County. At least one certainly did. Harvey Johnson had spent a few days with the Riders in Painesville on his way to freedom. He is said to have fallen in love with the pretty town, as well as appreciating the hospitality shown him. After the War, he made his way back to become our first Negro immigrant and lived here until he died aged 102.

LAKE COUNTY SPEAKS FOR UNION

On January 5, 1861, the U.S. ship *Star of the West* was fired on in Charleston harbor as it was bringing supplies to besieged Fort Sumter. This attack prompted Lake County community leaders to call a mass meeting of all citizens, regardless of political party, to consider "the perilous state of the Union." Enthusiasm and public sentiment were so strong that men unable to attend had to explain publicly the reason for their absence.

In Painesville's Courthouse those at the meeting agreed to do all possible "to preserve the present form of government" and "that prompt vigorous action alone could preserve the Union." Lake Countians indicated that they would rather lose their government than be found guilty of ignoring their obligation to it.

Soon after this patriotic meeting Lincoln himself came through Lake County on his way to Washington for his inauguration. Stopping ten minutes at the Painesville station on February 16, Lincoln spoke to a crowd of more than four thousand eager citizens. Reporting the event, the local press commented on his remarks and further observed "this man was not nearly as odd in appearance as previous reports had indicated."

WAR COMES TO LAKE COUNTY

Early in March, about the time of Lincoln's inauguration, another meeting was called in Painesville, this time to organize a militia company. Despite speeches by Judge Bissell, Jack Casement and other leading citizens, and a grand tone of patriotism, only four volunteers stepped forward to support the cause.

This apathy was erased dramatically, however, a few weeks later. On the morning of April 13 *Telegraph* handbills reported that Fort Sumter had been attacked. Within three days Lincoln called for 75,000 men. Lake Countians now set out in earnest to raise militia companies. They would "whip the Southern army, hang its traitors and anyone outside of the Confederacy who had assisted in this rebellion." "The Star Spangled Banner" was sung by church choirs at the beginning of church services. To the music of the Painesville Cornet Band, Lake County sent its first companies to answer the President's call, on April 30, 1861.

THE FIRST FAREWELLS

As was common in that day, the volunteer soldiers elected their officers as a part of the departure ceremony. Painesville and Concord's Union Guards elected John N. Dyer as captain, Perry-Madison volunteers chose E. A. Wright. The "Union Savers" from Mentor, Willoughby and Kirtland elected R. B. Moore of Willoughby. Leroy sent forty men led by Captain N. Carter.

Reporting to Camp Taylor in Cleveland, these first volunteers were re-assigned to regular units such as the Seventh Regiment, Ohio Volunteer Infantry. Painesville's Jack Casement was elected major of this regiment. After organization they went to Camp Dennison at Cincinnati.

Here they joined other Ohio units commanded by General George Mc-
Clellan, and, after brief training, marched into north-western Virginia
(now West Virginia) to meet the Confederates.

The Seventh's appetite for action was soon nourished. On June 3,
1861, units of McClellan's force fought Southern troops at Philippi.
Fighting another skirmish at Rich Mountain on July 11, McClellan's
army suffered a surprise attack and defeat at Cross Lanes, August 25.
Men of the Seventh and the people of Lake County were saddened by the
death in this battle of Painesville's popular John Dyer. The tragedy and
grief of war came home to Lake County all too soon.

BATTLEFIELD COMMITTEES

Following the battle at Cross Lanes, a committee was sent from Lake
County to look after the dead and wounded and to see that the proper
arrangements were made for their care. The dead were returned home
for burial, and the committee brought some of the more seriously
wounded back with them.

By the time of the Peninsular Campaign in 1862, citizen's committees
to care for the wounded were common on the battlefields. After the
battle at Shiloh, Mrs. B. O. Wilcox and Mrs. S. L. Noble told Lake County
of "the sorrowful scene of desolation" they saw, and the sacrifices the
soldiers had made. Although it was a truly humanitarian gesture, serving
with a battlefield committee was never a pleasant task.

OTHER MEN, OTHER BATTLES

In the course of the War, Lake County men served in approximately
sixty army units, infantry, artillery or cavalry. Some were in the United
States Navy, others fought with troops of other Union states. They were
on almost every front of action, in every major campaign or siege. Painesville's Band did regimental service through much of the War and was at
the front when it ended. Besides the Seventh OVI, three other units had
large representations from Lake County.

Recruited in the summer and autumn of 1861 at Cleveland's Camp
Wade, men of the Second Ohio Volunteer Cavalry saw action with three
Union army commands, all the way from Nevada, fighting Indians, to
the Atlantic Ocean. Men from Lake and Ashtabula Counties, recruited
by Joshua Giddings at Jefferson, served in the Twenty-ninth OVI in the
Shenandoah Valley campaigns of 1862, at Chancellorsville and Gettys-
burg in 1863. Late in 1863 they were reassigned to the Army of the
Cumberland and here joined with Lake County men of the 105th Ohio
Infantry.

By summer, 1862, it was clear to Lincoln that the war would be long
and difficult. In August Congress passed a Militia Act which called upon

the states to conscript men for the Army. Those of the 105th Ohio Infantry, from Lake and four other northeastern counties, were called "bounty" soldiers because each was paid $50 to volunteer. Lake County's quota was two hundred twenty men, and the County Commissioners voted to issue bonds to raise the necessary funds. Signed by many local citizens, these bonds produced the $11,000 to fill our quota. The 105th Infantry was the first regiment to leave Ohio under the Militia Act. It went into action with the Army of the Cumberland in Kentucky and Tennessee, and was with the army that captured Atlanta, and marched with General Sherman to the sea.

War service was not always at the front. Late in 1861 men were recruited here to guard Confederate prisoners on Sandusky's Johnson Island. Also two militia companies of five hundred men each were enlisted to serve as Home Guards. In the autumn of 1862 Governor Todd called for three hundred fifty men from Lake and Geauga Counties to meet the threat of Morgan's Raiders in southern Ohio. Although they saw no fighting and served only a short time, these "Squirrel Hunters," as they were nicknamed, were important emergency volunteers.

MORE RECRUITING AND CONSCRIPTION

In the early months of the war, Lake County was recognized as a fertile ground for volunteers, and even after Lincoln's draft order men continued to answer the call for action. By October 1862, Lake County could no longer fill its assigned quota with volunteers and had to turn to formal draft. In the summer of 1863 local merchants agreed to close their stores at 3 P. M. every day and devote the remainder of the day recruiting volunteers to stop Lee's invasion of the North.

The *Telegraph* in November 1863, announced another draft order calling for one hundred eighty-seven men from Lake County and warned that if this quota were not met, conscription would again be necessary. Recruiting was not going easily now, and big bounties were offered: $400 to a re-enlisting veteran, $300 to a volunteer, $100 to a draftee. Meetings were held in various communities in the winter of 1863-64 to raise the bounty money and fill the quota. Most of the funds came from private donation, and some individuals paid others to go as "substitute." By the fall of 1863, 1,500 men from Lake County were in service.

Some of the Lake County veterans were active in recruiting and were furloughed home for that purpose. Major Casement was quite successful in this work as were men of the Second Cavalry and Twenty-ninth Infantry. Some were returned home to recruit for their units in the spring of 1864, and most of them were able to fill their quotas. Manpower at home was decreasing steadily as more stepped forward to fill the ranks of fallen veterans.

THE HOMEFRONT

Rare was the home in Lake County that didn't feel some effects of the War. Almost everyone knew the absence of loved ones, many suffered the grief of loss. As the men marched to camp and on to battle, our communities organized to support our soldiers.

While their volunteer company was forming in the spring of 1861, Perry and Madison women devoted a day or two a week to making wool shirts and other clothing for the new soldiers. At the same time, citizens of Lake County began collecting food and other items and sent them to men in camp. One of the first of these shipments contained 250 pounds of butter, 180 bushels of potatoes, 100 pounds of cheese, 200 pounds of dried apples, a barrel of eggs, cheese cakes, sweetmeats, biscuits, socks and more clothing. More of an individual gesture at first, women soon grouped together to can food, knit and sew for their absent menfolk.

THE SOLDIERS' AID SOCIETY

In October 1861, Lake County organized a Soldiers' Aid Society "for relief of the sick and wounded of the Federal Army" and "to gather and prepare hospital supplies for the front." This group collected blankets, cotton bandages, medicines, socks, yarn and dried apples, and directed their shipment to the soldiers. The Aid Society soon became a project in which nearly all the people were involved — man, woman and child — and its work continued up to the close of the War.

All Soldiers' Aid Societies in the country eventually became part of the United States Sanitary Commission (forerunner of our present American Red Cross). A history of its activities in northern Ohio during the War says, "The Painesville Branch, one of the most valued tributaries of the Cleveland Sanitary Commission, has furnished no estimate of its large contributions. Its members were unwearied in their work through the whole course of the war, and in addition to their usual supplies were notably active in preparing canned fruit and vegetables and blackberry cordial through the summer months. They responded with great promptness to any call for hospital stores, and constantly followed with their gifts those regiments that had enlisted from Lake County."

Many were the ways in which the Aid Societies raised money for the soldiers. One of the greatest efforts was Cleveland's Sanitary Fair in February 1864. It was opened with speeches by northern Ohio's leading citizens, including General James A. Garfield. Decorations in Lake County's booth were described as "elaborate and tasteful," and its shelves were filled with "beautiful needlework, designs in [pine] cones and mosses, models, toys and embroideries." In the Fine Arts Hall two of

James Beard's studies of animals were on display with other popular contemporary art works. The Painesville Society furnished part of the evening entertainment with "A Continental Tea Party," tea served by ladies in costume and setting of Revolutionary times. This single affair raised $1,600 for soldier relief.

WAR NEWS

The people at home were constantly looking for word of their soldiers in action. Any news was eagerly sought, and the morale of Lake County rose or fell with the fortunes of the Union Army. The *Telegraph* gave full reports of troops in camp and battle, frequently publishing letters from the soldiers. As the account of Cross Lanes had shocked Lake Countians, news of victory at Antietam revived them. After victories at Gettysburg and Vicksburg, our communities celebrated a Day of National Thanksgiving August 6, 1863. Stores were closed. Painesville Congregationalists, Methodists and Disciples of Christ met for a united service in the new First Church.

Families always welcomed happily the soldiers home on leave. Army hospital facilities were so limited that many soldiers were able to return home to recover. A more cheerful occupation for the soldiers' families was providing entertainment for men on furlough. Late in 1863 some local citizens even wrote Secretary of War Edwin Stanton requesting leave for the veterans of the Seventh OVI. Men of the Second Cavalry were entertained with a fine dinner at the Cowles House in Painesville while others enjoyed a dance at the Parmly House. In January 1864, Colonel Jack Casement was welcomed home as he came to report to the families of men in his command.

WAR'S OTHER EFFECTS AT HOME

Absent men meant many Lake County homes and farms were without their essential labor force. Many families learned sacrifice at first hand with shortages of food and resources. Staple foods became scarce and costly as more and more goods were sent to the troops. In a few months of the winter 1862-63, prices for wheat, oats and corn went up as did flour, potatoes and apples. Prices for cotton cloth doubled in the same period. In a generous gesture to aid those families financially burdened, Dr. Andrews Merriman of Madison offered his professional services free to all families whose husband had gone to War. About his community, Painesville's C. S. Leonard wrote to soldier Lafayette Blair in February 1863, "War is the ruin of some and some the making of."

MONUMENTS AND HEROES

As early as October 1862, a *Telegraph* editorial called for a county war memorial because "this terrible rebellion is touching the heart of every household in the land." Painesville's War Monument and those in other communities eloquently remind us of the full sacrifice made by many of our native sons. Among the names are the plain soldiers who fought to preserve the Union. Among the names also are some who came out of the smoke of battle to rise to even greater heights in service to their communities and nation. One of these was James Abram Garfield.

Chapter XIII

Politics and Politicians

Our early political life was described by S. S. Osborn in a letter he wrote in 1900. Recalling the old days, when he first came into the County, Osborn said, "In 1827 Capt. [Edward] Paine [Jr.] was clerk of the County. His relative Eleazer Paine . . . was County Auditor. Sylvestor N. Hoyt, brother-in-law of Eleazer Paine, was County Treasurer, and Alfred Phelps, brother-in-law of Capt. Paine, Deputy Clerk. The Paine family controlled & had for years the offices of the County. They were good and competent men, the only objection was bossism . . ." In 1820 and again in 1824, "John Hubbard of Madison broke into the ring and was elected to the Legislature . . . That was before the day of conventions and parties. It was the Paine party and the Hubbard party but each man was an independent candidate." This pattern of local politics lasted a good many years.

NATIONAL CAMPAIGNS

Not until 1840 were there political campaigns in Lake County like the ones we know today. Great enthusiasm was built up for William Henry Harrison in a crusade of the West against the East. Harrison had won the Battle of the Thames during the War of 1812 and, the westerners believed, saved the frontier. He was one of them, a frontier hero. His Whig supporters turned a sneering jibe of the Van Buren men into one of the most exciting, colorful campaigns in the history of our country. The Democrats had said of Harrison, "Give him a barrel of hard cider and he will sit the remainder of his days, content, in a log cabin." So log cabins and hard cider came to symbolize the contest in newspaper cartoons, on Whig campaign buttons, in song and reality.

On October 5, 1840, Lake County celebrated the anniversary of the Battle of the Thames. The *Telegraph* reported, "Two grand processions from the east and the west met at the principal corners of the streets of our village and passed each other in fine style, countermarching and meeting again on the public square . . . Madison as usual excelled in immense vehicles, streaming banners and fine ladies. LeRoy [sic] was here en masse, in most imposing array. Willoughby and Mentor sent its multitude of enthusiastic Whigs and Buckeye girls to animate and grace the scene. Kirtland, Concord and Perry were scarcely behind the other townships in their contributions to honor the day and give interest to the occasion." From 11 a. m. to nearly 5 p. m. the crowd gathered around the log cabin on the square to hear speeches and to sing. "The day was delightful — all hearts were full of animation and hope — no accident occurred to mar the general joy — everything passed off in good taste and good order."

Needless to add, the Whigs carried Lake County.

CIVIC LEADERS

Through the years the majority of Lake Countians voted for Whig candidates and later, Republicans. Many fine men have represented us in our State and Federal legislatures. Though some of these leaders were not from our own county, there was an intimacy throughout the Reserve in the days of a much smaller population, and these men were as familiar to our residents as they were to their own neighbors. Men like Peter Hitchcock, Elisha Whittlesey, Joshua Giddings, Benjamin Wade and James Garfield were our friends and we were proud to watch them secure for Ohio and the nation a firm foundation of law and order at a most vital time in our development.

PETER HITCHCOOK

Peter Hitchcook of Burton entered public life in 1810 and served our communities for over forty years. He started as our district's State Representative, became State Senator in 1812 and Representative to United States Congress in 1817. Two years later he was elected Judge of the Supreme Court of Ohio.

When Judge Hitchcook first started his career, Ohio was sparsely populated and still a frontier state. He worked in the unsettled conditions of a rapidly growing population as two million people poured into Ohio from the eastern seaboard and Europe. In this ever-changing scene, he did more than any other man in the state to establish our Ohio Court on an efficient, sound and practical basis. It was said by those who knew him that "he was endowed by nature with calm self-possession, firmness of purpose, and self-reliant judgment" and "he improved upon these faculties by constant habits of sobriety, personal restraint and untiring industry." On his way from a court session, he died in Painesville at the home of his son, Reuben Hitchcook.

ELISHA WHITTLESEY

Elisha Whittlesey came to Canfield (now Mahoning County) in 1807 and opened a law office there. It was not long before he became well known, and many aspiring young men went to study with him. He was elected to the Ohio Legislature in 1820 and, as our Representative, to Congress in 1822. It was Whittlesey who was responsible for obtaining the $1000 appropriation to complete Fairport's harbor. Serving eight terms, he resigned in 1837 to take on other government assignments. He was Comptroller of the Treasury under Presidents Taylor, Fillmore, Pierce and Lincoln. Whittlesey was one of the most beloved men of the Western Reserve and one of the ablest in Congress during his service there. The term "Watchdog of the Treasury" was applied to him derisively by his political opponents, but with infinite respect by his many friends.

JOSHUA R. GIDDINGS

The Giddings family were early settlers in Wayne (Ashtabula County), where Joshua grew up in the pioneer life of the Western Reserve. When he was twenty-one he began studying law in the office of Elisha Whittlesey and was admitted to the Bar in 1812. He set up his practice in Jefferson, the County seat, and soon won confidence for his skill and care in preparing his cases and for his forceful and logical presentation. When Whittlesey resigned from Congress, Giddings was elected to the vacancy.

For twenty-one years through the growing dissension between northern and southern states, Giddings upheld anti-slavery principles in Congress when there was none but John Quincy Adams to support him. He and Adams joined together in 1837 to work for the repeal of the "Gag" Rule which tabled all petitions concerning slavery without reading, reference or debate. They both struck a blow for the abolition of slavery in the District of Columbia at every opportunity.

Giddings was "bold, determined and fearless, saying little in the House except when the subject of slavery arose — then always on his feet." His district certainly approved of his views for they elected him again and again. Owing to a breakdown in his health he did not run in 1858. In 1861 Lincoln offered him the Consul-Generalship of Canada, and Giddings died in Montreal three years later in the midst of his duties. In private life he loved sports, music and children. His letters to his own children reveal a charming understanding, sympathy and mutual confidence.

BENJAMIN FRANKLIN WADE

Benjamin Wade as a young man of twenty-one came with his family to Andover, Ashtabula County, and helped his father clear a farm. He, too, studied law with Whittlesey and was admitted to the Bar of

Jefferson in 1827. He soon became a partner of Giddings, and they established their reputations together, as well as developing their philosophy of abolition together. In 1837 Wade was elected to the Ohio Senate, serving two terms before he was made presiding Judge of the Common Pleas Court. In 1851 he became our United States Senator and soon made his mark as an anti-slavery leader. "Of all men, Wade was most feared, trusted and respected by his political opponents." He impressed all who heard him, and he rarely made an enemy, although he so belligerently opposed slavery.

When Lincoln died, Wade was regarded as head of the Republican party. When Andrew Johnson became President, Wade was made President pro-tempore of the Senate. In this office he presided at the trial for the impeachment of Johnson. In 1869 Wade returned to his law office in Jefferson, although he remained active in the Republican party at local, state and national levels until his death in 1878.

JAMES ABRAM GARFIELD

James A. Garfield was already a well known figure when he bought a farm in Mentor in 1876. As a minister of the Disciple Church, he had often visited the Mentor pulpit as well as those in other towns of the Reserve. He was Representative to Congress from this area and was even more closely tied to our community because he had spent a number of summers on Little Mountain. Mentor welcomed a distinguished new citizen, already an old friend.

Garfield was born November 19, 1831, in a humble log cabin in Orange Township, Cuyahoga County. His father died before he was two, leaving his mother with four children to raise on a partially cleared farm. By selling part of the land, she was able to keep the family together. Even with all his chores, young Garfield became an insatiable reader. His cousins on a neighboring farm supplied him with books and companionship in his search for knowledge.

He first attended a nearby district school, went on to Geauga Seminary of Chester, Ohio, and in 1851 entered the Eclectic Institute (today's Hiram College). To pay for his education he worked on the Ohio Canal, as a carpenter and as a district school teacher. He graduated from Williams College in Massachusetts in 1856, returned to Hiram to teach and soon became principal there. It was during this time that he married Lucretia Rudolph, a Hiram resident and fellow student.

Serving two years as Ohio Senator before the Civil War came, Garfield entered service as Lt. Colonel, 42nd Regiment, OVI, and saw action in Kentucky and at the battles of Shiloh and Chickamauga. He became the youngest Major General in the Northern Army, but his military career was cut short by his election to the U. S. House of Representatives in 1863. He reluctantly left the army upon urging by Lincoln to go to Washington. In 1880 as Senator-elect from Ohio, he won the Republican nomination for the Presidency and the next year became the twentieth President of the United States.

In the meantime the Garfield family arrived on their farm in 1877. This was the first home that really satisfied Garfield's tastes. It was to him a place "where my boys can learn to work and where I can myself have some exercise, where I can touch the earth and get some strength from it." He plowed, drove oxen and helped with the harvest with keen zest.

The Garfields enlarged the farmhouse to a two-and-a-half story structure with a wide open porch across the front. This is famed as the site of the first and certainly one of the most successful "front porch campaigns" for the Presidency. Garfield traveled very little during the summer and fall of 1880, but a steady stream of visitors proved he was a tremendously popular candidate. The Lake Shore Railroad ran special excursion trains on tracks that crossed the farm, and a stop was arranged at a cow lane leading to Lawnfield, the Garfield home. Campaign headquarters were in a small outbuilding where a clicking telegraph key reported the latest developments across the nation. Here Garfield received the word that he had won the election.

His term of office was tragically short. On July 2, 1881, Garfield was shot in the Washington railroad station by Charles Guiteau, an office seeker disappointed by Garfield's firm support of the new civil service law. The wound itself was not fatal, but infection set in and on September 19 he died, our second martyred and much mourned President.

His life was crowded with accomplishments. He had been student, teacher, college president, minister, Army general, local and national government officer. Theodore Clark Smith, in his biography, says of Garfield, "Up to the end he was the man of affection, of sympathy, of courage; the leader desirous of agreement rather than conflict; the clear-eyed and open-minded thinker on political problems and not the dominating master on the one hand or the idealistic reformer on the other . . . Broken short as it was, his career has that completeness that inheres in a life lived consistently and unflinchingly in the light of reason and kindness."

Chapter XIV

Men at Work

The decades after the Civil War saw many rapid changes in the pattern of American life. The Industrial Revolution moved out of childhood into its teens. Cities mushroomed. Great fortunes rocketed, while the poor were often very poor. But this national trend hardly seemed to touch Lake County. We remained primarily an agricultural society. No booming industries, no overgrown cities, no spectacular wealth, no squalid slums developed here. Our significant changes were almost hidden amid the quiet and comfortable life of steadily increasing prosperity for the farmer and the small town shopkeeper. Seeds of progress were here, nevertheless. They were present in every phase of our working life, on the farms, in our industries, for men, women and children. In this chapter we shall watch these seeds grow into the harvest of the Twentieth Century.

SPECIALIZED AGRICULTURE

When the early settlers cleared their farms, their first crops were subsistence food for their families. As neighbors came, one man's surplus yield could be traded for another man's specialty. It might be a wheel of cheese from a cow owner, venison from an expert hunter, or tuition for a few weeks schooling for the children from an educated young lady. After the Erie and Ohio Canals were open and the railroad came, better transportation and new markets encouraged single crop agriculture and quantity shipping. The farmer began to consider what was the best paying crop for his soil, this climate and his particular skills.

Our first surveyors recognized that good soil lay beneath the virgin forest leaves. Luxurious growth of many trees and plants gave evidence of well-watered and naturally drained sand, clay and loam — a variety of soil to encourage a variety of crops.

The first few growing seasons gave the pioneers experience with our climate. Our temperature is influenced by our position between Lake Erie and the last ridge of the Appalachian Mountains. In the spring, ice on the Lake tends to keep the land cool and the fruit buds tight until danger of late frost is over. During summer, cool air from the higher land rolls down after dark to the warm Lake. These comfortable nights bring dew which promotes good pasture grass. As a result of these natural factors, it became evident to the farmers that orchards and dairies were reliable sources of income.

FRUIT GROWING

Turhand Kirtland had written in his diary on June 3, 1798: "Arrived at Grand River, encamped, found . . . as fine large strawberries as ever I saw." John Melish, an Irishman visiting the United States in 1811, wrote in his diary of his stop at Chagrin River on October 25: "Here we found a fine farm, and an orchard well stocked with fruit-trees." Eber Howe and later editors of the *Telegraph* often reported on the size and taste of fruit brought in by their subscribers. As early as 1847, fruit was an important export from Fairport. In that year alone 2,700 barrels of dried fruit brought into the county $32,832.

In Perry, the cider and vinegar mill of Nelson House was the largest in northern Ohio. He sold 4,000 barrels of vinegar in the east in 1876. Grapes did very well on our lake slopes too. The Shakers from North Union Village (now Shaker Heights) had extensive vineyards near Worden Road (now Wickliffe) and maintained a warehouse at the railroad. Apples, peaches, plums and pears, as well as a variety of berries, were profitable crops.

"CHEESEDOM"

Mid-nineteenth century was the height of dairy farming. At this time the Western Reserve was known as "Cheesedom." Practically every locality had at least one factory which took in the milk from 100 to 500 cows daily and transformed it into more easily transportable cheese. In 1847, 1,131,107 pounds of cheese and 308,870 pounds of butter were exported from Fairport. By 1876 cheese production had dropped, but milk and cream in large quantities went to Cleveland and New York by the Lake Shore Railroad. Dairying remained an important part of the county's economy for many years.

HELP FROM MACHINERY

During these years, the second half of the nineteenth century, farm equipment changed dramatically. Cast iron plows were replaced by sharper and stronger steel ones. Corn planters and wheat drills did away with the drudgery of sowing by hand. Mowing machines became practical. Threshers, used to beat the grain from the stalks, were cumbersome but could do the work of many men in shorter time. They were operated by a steam engine and were usually owned by one man in the neighborhood who moved his machine and gang to one farm after another.

A. E. Vrooman, raised on Dock Road in Madison, developed an onion topper which he and his father manufactured in Painesville. It was the first practical machine of this type to be patented and put on the market, and was a great labor saving device. Lake County became the first area in the state to produce onions for shipment. Men continued to explore the profitable possibilities of our rich soil and good growing climate.

NURSERIES

In 1854, Jesse Storrs of Courtland County, New York, bought eighty acres in Painesville Township and planted a few of these to trees. From this small beginning Storrs' business grew to be the largest departmental nursery in the United States. Fruit trees, ornamental shrubs and vines, evergreens, roses, perennials, annual flower and vegetable seeds were all sold by Storrs and the partner who joined him, James J. Harrison. Here many early Lake County nurserymen served their apprenticeships and learned their skills. When these employees had saved a little capital, they started their own nurseries. In this way Lake County nursery business continues to expand into the Twentieth Century.

KNOW-HOW DEVELOPS

Farmers have always felt the need to discuss mutual problems with each other. In 1823 a Geauga County Agricultural Society was formed to provide an exchange of information. Men from what is now Lake County played an important part in the organization's development, and they promoted the annual fair, the first in the State, held on Chardon Square. A newly formed Lake County Society purchased its own fairground in Painesville in 1852. These fairs encouraged competition in agricultural arts and the advance of new ideas in farming methods and techniques.

Another important function was performed by the Granges, founded in all our townships between 1874 and 1876. The Grange, officially called the Patrons of Husbandry, was initiated by a clerk in the United States Department of Agriculture in 1867. Among the pioneers active in this movement was Anson Bartlett of North Madison. He not only started branches, but he also helped to shape the national policy of the organization.

Seeking to improve the farmer's economic position, the Grange worked for lower freight rates for the small shipper. It made politicians aware of farmers' interests and did influence some legislation. However, its real contribution was as a cultural and educational society which made the farmer less isolated, enlarged his vision and gave him a feeling of importance as one of a group.

IMPROVING THE SOIL

In the early days the virgin soil was rich with the accumulation of centuries of leaf mulch. Gradually the continuation of crops began to use up this wealth. In the spring of 1869 Charles Ruggles introduced net fishing at Fairport, and the first season he caught fifteen hundred sturgeon. There was no market for them as food, so he sold them to Storrs and Harrison at a dollar a wagonload, the first recorded commercial fertilizer in the county. Before the century was over, fertilizers of all kinds were being imported and used with care to improve Lake County's soil. Our farmers were learning to make better use of their land.

Proper drainage of the land was another problem of the farmer. To be able to work a field earlier in the spring, to avoid water standing on young crops and turning the soil sour, it is necessary to have some form of drainage on most land. Simple drains were made by cutting saplings, laying them in a ditch below the depth of a plow and then shoveling earth back over them. These were unsatisfactory because wood soon rots. Gradually the farmers turned to draining with tile. This idea developed a market for one of our first modern industries.

J. W. PENFIELD AND SON

As a young boy J. W. Penfield had come with his family to Willoughby Township in 1834 and helped improve their farm on the site of Pine Ridge Country Club, Wickliffe. He grew up familiar with such problems as good drainage and built his first machine to make drain tiles in 1853. It was exhibited at several fairs and won many prizes and medals. The business grew and in 1872 J. W. Penfield built the factory still standing at the east end of Pelton Street bridge in Willoughby. Here he not only made tile but he supplied other factories with the machinery to make tile. This transition, from selling a simple product to selling the machinery to make the product, marks the Penfields' factory as "modern industry," quite different from our early mills.

THE EFFECT OF STEAM

The Industrial Revolution of the Nineteenth Century was based on steam power. No longer was it necessary for a mill to shut down during the summer dry spells or winter freeze-ups. No longer was it necessary for a man to own land on a stream to build a factory. With steam power harnessed, men's ingenuity burst into great creative activity. More and more machines were developed to make more and more articles with less and less man-effort, and at less cost. Northeastern Ohio became, and has continued to be, a center for the manufacture of fine machinery. Lake County has played its part in establishing that reputation.

COE-WILKES COMPANY

In 1851 H. H. Coe and Leonard Anderson of Painesville formed a partnership to make steam engines and sawmill machinery. They built a plant at Jackson and St. Clair Streets and prospered for ten years, finding a market for their equipment in lumber mills throughout the Reserve. After running the business alone for several years while Coe fought with the Northern Army, Anderson sold his interest to Frederick Wilkes.

The new partner was an engineer and a practical business man. Wilkes had worked in the 1830's as a clerk at Arcole Furnace. In 1845 with John Wilkeson, son of one of the proprietors of Arcole, he built an iron furnace at Lowell, Ohio, on the Mahoning River. Here they were among the first to use successfully raw coal instead of charcoal in the smelting process. Wilkes later returned to Lake County, converted Geauga Furnace to coal and then joined H. H. Coe.

At about this time natural gas was discovered in Lake County in sufficiently wide pockets to serve as fuel for gas lights on many farms. Town street lighting by artificial gas also became common, and the picturesque lamplighter made his rounds at dusk with his ladder under his arm and a burning taper in hand.

This opened up a new market for the Coe-Wilkes Company to produce a machine that could cut thin stock from giant logs. The owners improved the rotary type lathe which Anderson had first invented. This, together with a clipper machine, made the narrow tapers every lamplighter and every householder needed. The first lathes and clippers were installed in 1870 in a plant owned by Charles Pratt on the west bank of Grand River on what is now the south side of Route 84. The location was known for many years as Toothpick Hill, for the factory soon found this other product could also be made with the fine precision machinery of the Coe-Wilkes Company.

In 1891 Wilkes retired, Coe's son Henry joined the business and the company adopted its present name, Coe Manufacturing. As the forests diminished, the rotary lathe entered a new market producing veneer, and later plywood. The company's leading position in these industries was made possible by H. H. Coe's roller drier, built in 1902. It was the first machine in which veneer was moved along as it dried and was delivered in a continuous operation. Here was an early step in Twentieth Century automation.

COAL AND IRON

We have already seen in the early days a mill or a shipyard did not long remain independent of other industries. One business both attracted and depended on others. As the Industrial Age developed, factories became part of an area, rather than a local, concentration. We found ourselves in a community encompassing Cleveland, Akron, Pittsburgh and Erie. All grew together, their products and facilities complementing each other. It was this area development which created our role in the great coal and iron industry.

In August 1855, the schooner *Columbia,* one of the first ships through the new Sault St. Marie Canal, brought to Cleveland one hundred thirty-two tons of iron ore from the rich beds on Lake Superior. Her arrival was hardly noted among the ships of that day, but the voyage marked the beginning of a huge business. Cleveland and Pittsburgh vied for leadership. One was closer to the supply of ore, the other to the coal fields in southern Ohio and West Virginia.

Pittsburgh, realizing that it needed improved transportation south from the Lake, chose Fairport as a likely harbor. In 1885 Henry W. Oliver arrived in Lake County to begin plans for construction of larger docks, dredging a deeper channel and extending the railroad.

NEW LIFE AT FAIRPORT

After the coming of the Lake Shore Railroad, Fairport had gradually lost its importance as a harbor. The prosperous ship-provisioning business dropped off as well as the handling of imports and exports. For a decade the town's chief industry was a nitroglycerine factory in two warehouses on the pier, owned by J. H. King, C. M. Wheeler and H. Hinkley. They built storage facilities on the west bank and shipped explosives to the ore mines on Lake Superior and to the oil fields in Pennsylvania.

A terrific explosion in the storehouse wrecked the factory on November 1, 1870. Many homes in the village were practically ruined and every window in town was broken. The owners promptly and generously made good on the damages claimed by the citizens, but the factory was not rebuilt.

A railroad from Fairport to Hudson had been incorporated in 1852, but had never extended beyond one stone viaduct (still standing) south of Painesville. A narrow gauge line, the Painesville and Youngstown Railroad, was built in 1871, but there was not enough additional money to improve the docks, so that this railroad did not add to Fairport's prosperity.

It was Henry W. Oliver, and the capital from Pittsburgh which he represented, that put new life into Fairport. After 1885 not only were new docks constructed, but the old railroad was rebuilt to standard gauge, with necessary bridges, water tanks and sidings, and extended to Pittsburgh. There was more work than men available, and this labor need was soon filled by a wave of immigration from Europe.

THE SLOVAKS

From the northeastern boundary of old Hungary, the Slovaks were a minority group, forced to follow Hungarian patterns. They appreciated the opportunities of American freedom, rapidly becoming citizens of their new country.

Paul Locotosh is credited with being the first Slovak to arrive in Fairport. He came in 1883 and was soon followed by Michael Pillar, Mike Benedict, John Kocak and Mike Petro. The men worked on the docks, supplying their own picks and shovels and using wheelbarrows to unload ore from the boats. They saved their earnings until they could send for their wives and children. They were joined by more of their countrymen as the activity on the docks increased. These Slovak families formed a little colony on Water Street between Second Street and the Lake, and this area continues to be the center of their community.

THE FINNS

The first Finns came to Fairport to work on widening the Painesville and Youngstown Railroad. They started on the project in Youngstown under foreman Charles Hilston, a Finnish immigrant of 1873, and when the road was finished at Fairport, many of them stayed to work on the docks. By 1887 there were about two hundred men and a few of their wives and children. Some of our early Finnish leaders were Kalle Helstein, William Hirvi, Mikko Pohto, John Ollila, Matti Killinen, Isaac Ronni, Jacob Kupari and Niiles Katila.

Many of these new arrivals came from the Vaasa Province on the Gulf of Bothnia, known as the "breadbasket" of Finland. The law of primogeniture, whereby the land was always inherited by the oldest son, sent many younger sons of these farm families to seek opportunity in America. In Finland they had been used to strenuous outdoor labor, and they worked here on the ore docks in summer and at lumbering in the winter. They soon realized that they were in a land of opportunity and of privilege as well. They themselves could do something about making life more pleasant and more worthwhile. They worked for law and order and were strong advocates of temperance.

THE HUNGARIANS

Most of the Hungarians who came to Fairport at the end of the Nineteenth Century were from the neighborhood of Nagy Kapos, an area now under the domination of Czechoslovakia. The distant cousins of our Hungarian citizens are now suffering from the same restrictions which led our early Slovaks to emigrate.

Frank Wayner and Mike Bartish arrived in Fairport in 1889 and are said to be the first of their nationality here. They were soon joined by more of their countrymen. Following the custom of the other immigrants, they worked hard, saved their earnings and sent for their wives, or returned home in the winter to find a wife. They were a neat and thrifty people, gay and emotional, and soon learned English to become a part of our American scene. They were good cooks and their national favorites, cabbage rolls and chicken paprikas, have become popular American foods. Their folk dances and music continue to enliven Fairport festivals.

NEW CHURCHES

With these people came new religious backgrounds. They quite naturally wished to worship in their own language following their own customs. In the early 1890's three churches, known today as Zion Lutheran, Immanuel Lutheran and First Evangelical Lutheran, were established by the Finnish people.

The Hungarians and many of the Slovaks joined with the English-speaking Roman Catholics to form St. Anthony's Church, completing their building in 1899. St. Michael's Greek Catholic Church, which serves another group of Slovaks, was built in 1926.

WOMEN AT WORK

Not only was the Industrial Revolution changing agriculture and industry and bringing new nationalities to our doorstep, but it was also affecting woman's role in society. Iron stoves, crude washing machines, carpet sweepers and running water in the house began to lighten her tasks. The Painesville Steam Laundry, opened in 1887, brought a further aid to housekeeping. More homes too could afford a hired girl, either from a less prosperous farm or from the new immigrant families. Women began to have leisure to devote to community improvement.

There had been a few early attempts to encourage temperance. They were not very successful in pioneer society where there was little else to offer one's guests but a drink of whiskey. But it was not until after the Civil War that women banded together to work for prohibition. Painesville's branch of the Women's Temperance Union was begun in 1874. This group opened a reading room where young men could find recreation as a substitute for an evening in a local saloon. The reading room operated for twenty-five years until the books were turned over to start a public library.

EQUAL RIGHTS ASSOCIATION

H. C. Gray of Willoughby was the first advocate of women's suffrage in Lake County and one of the first in the state. He was a member of the State Constitution Convention of 1851 where he proposed legislation for women's suffrage. He found no support. His fellow citizen G. W. Clement met with more interest in 1880 when he introduced a bill in the Ohio Legislature to allow women to vote for members of school boards and to serve as members of such boards. But interest was not great enough to pass the bill.

In 1883 a group of prominent and influential women, under the leadership of Mrs. Frances J. Casement, formed a local branch of the Equal Rights Association. Mrs. Casement became president of the state organization in 1885. She was an inveterate letter writer and, with dogged determination, won support and workers for the cause. Mrs. Martha H. Elwell of Willoughby later carried on the crusade in the county and state.

Through efforts of the Association, the laws governing property rights were changed so that women could stand on an equality with men in business matters. Their leaders urged women to take part in government and worked to convince men that women should do so. Finally in 1895 women did obtain the right to vote for school board members, and in that year two women were elected to the Painesville Board of Education.

OUR PUBLIC SCHOOLS

The children's world was changing also. While the foundation for our school system had been laid well before the Civil War, it required many years of discussion, experimentation and more legislation to put theories into effect.

Painesville had created in 1851 a Board of Education, which established graded classes through high school, and had taxed her citizens to provide free education for all, adequate buildings and acceptable salaries. Other communities followed suit, although only furnishing eight grades. Mentor Village organized its Union School in 1863, Madison and Willoughby in 1867. Madison Seminary and Willoughby Collegiate Institute continued to supply high school courses.

THOMAS HARVEY

Our outstanding figure in public education at this time was Thomas Harvey. He was appointed superintendent of Painesville schools in 1865 and served until 1881, except for six years spent at Columbus as State Supervisor. He had come to Painesville as a boy of twelve and had been printer's apprentice on the *Telegraph* for six years. He then studied at

Kirtland's Western Reserve Teachers' Seminary, organized a high school at Chardon, and supervised Massillon's schools for fourteen years. Harvey was a thoughtful, experienced educator with integrity and devotion to his profession. He was known throughout the state for his effective leadership in advancing the cause of better public schools and he made a national reputation with his series of *Grammars*. His influence was felt in all the County, as well as in Painesville.

MORE ADVANCES IN PUBLIC EDUCATION

The old tendency to let each community go its own way, inherited from the frontier days, was not easy to overcome. Changes came slowly, but dissatisfaction with the condition of rural schools grew under Harvey's interest and leadership. In 1877 Mentor Township residents petitioned the state for permission to form a Special School District. This was one of the first Ohio areas outside of incorporated towns to achieve a graded school. It was not until 1900 that grading became compulsory throughout the state and the life of the one-room schoolhouse was over.

Another step toward improved education was made in 1877 when school attendance was required by law. Gone were the days when boys such as Henry Jones of Wickliffe could be kept at home to scare the deer off his father's wheat field. All children from eight to fourteen, and their parents, were now subject to the truant officer. Six years of schooling were assured.

More improvements were still needed. For many years education above the eighth grade could be had only in the larger towns. The children from rural areas had to pay tuition and transportation, and usually room and board as well. The coming of the street car gave many a chance to attend high school in Willoughby, Painesville or Madison. But until 1921 it remained more difficult for a country boy or girl to obtain the last four years of public school education, which today we take for granted, than it is for anyone in Lake County to go to college now.

LAKE ERIE FEMALE SEMINARY

The new Lake Erie Female Seminary opened its doors in Painesville in September 1859. Its trustees — Reuben Hitchcock, Aaron Wilcox, Charles A. Avery, Silas T. Ladd, Timothy Rockwell and William L. Perkins — were all outstanding leaders in the community. Financial problems during the War tested their courage, but with Principal Lydia A. Sessions, they met the emergency and were in good operating condition when the War ended.

Misses Mary A. Evans and Luella Bentley became Principal and Assistant Principal in 1868, and their personalities molded forty years of students. Gracious, always ladylike, with twinkling eyes, they managed trustees, faculty, janitors, girls (and their beaus) with intelligent ease. Quotations from early catalogues reveal the educational philosophy of this capable pair.

"All the teachers and students board in the Seminary. . . . No day students are admitted. This is for the sake of carrying on the school work with less interruption, and especially on account of the domestic situation, which admits of no privileged class exempt from the common duties and responsibilities of the one family. The ordinary daily house-work. . . . gives healthful exercise, cultivates a taste for home occupations, honors labor. . . ."

By 1897, "The Seminary, by a natural and unforced growth of many years, has reached a college standard in the requirements for admission to the regular course of study. . . . in the age and maturity of its students and in the scholarly aims and methods of its instructors. . . . It is the constant aim to develop character founded upon Christian principle and to prepare for the duties of Christian womanhood." The standards of the school continued to rise and the next year the Seminary became Lake Erie College, with the power to confer degrees.

THE MATHEWS SCHOOL

Mrs. Samuel Mathews, daughter-in-law of Painesville's pioneer doctor, started a school in her home, primarily as a preparatory school for Lake Erie Seminary. In *Kathie's Diary*, one of the students describes it, "Its [sic] in a lovely old fashioned house with lots of interesting old time furniture. . . . Mrs. Mayhew [sic] is a lovely lady and a fine teacher. . . . Dr. Mayhew [sic] is real jolly and teaches Latin so its [sic] very interesting." The school took both day pupils and out-of-state boarding students for nearly thirty years, closing its doors in 1900.

MEN AT WORK ELSEWHERE

During the last half of the Nineteenth Century census figures show a drop in our rural areas, but all over the country this was happening. Better farm equipment meant fewer hands needed and fewer jobs available. Young men went to the cities to seek their fortunes in the expanding industries. Fortunately, many of them remembered their childhood home.

They returned for summer holidays and brought back a flavor of city sophistication. Much wealth in the county is a result of an uncle's or brother's investment in a native son's enterprise elsewhere. Our ties with the world strengthened through these emigrants. They, in turn, as had Dan Beard, spread their Lake County heritage to other parts of the country.

FREDERICK BURR OPPER

One of our native sons was Frederick Burr Opper, born in Madison in 1857. He early showed his skill with a pencil and the Beard brothers encouraged him to support himself with his special talent. For fifteen years he did cartoons for *Puck* magazine in New York, until in the 1890's he sold his idea of a strip cartoon to the Hearst newspapers.

Magazines and newspapers had for many years used cartoons to make fun of political party differences, to explain policies, to defend issues and to expose wrongs. New was the idea of a series of pictures to tell an amusing story and to depict a colorful character. This is what Opper offered to Hearst.

Opper's figures were energetic and full of life. "Maud," the mule, was strenuous; "Alphonse and Gaston" were always trying to outdo each other; "Happy Hooligan" cavorted through one absurd situation after another. All had individuality. For thirty years they continued to bring fun to children and adults. Opper was the dean of comic supplement artists, both by age and reputation. His creations were the forerunners of an American institution, the Sunday "funnies."

Men like Frederick Opper reflected another change in our way of living in the Post-Civil War days. In settled communities, where frontier hardships were now just memories, the ease and convenience of daily life were accepted matters of fact. Men's leisure and means contributed to a growing awareness of Lake County's most enduring inheritance — the natural beauty of our countryside.

Chapter XV

Our Continuing Resource

As we read of the hardships endured and the enormous amount of work accomplished by our pioneers, we are apt to think they had little pleasure and less leisure. Such is not the case for they often made of their work an opportunity for a social gathering. They helped each other with house-building and barn-raising, with harvesting and husking. The women too enjoyed quilting bees and apple butter parties. Going to mill was a social event. If times were not too busy, the whole family went to hear the miller's news and to chat with neighbors along the way.

It was not long before picnics were planned to enjoy the broad sands, wide-open sky and beautiful sunsets across Lake Erie, or to explore the rocks and caves under the mammoth pines and hemlocks of Little Mountain. The residents found pleasure in the beauties of our landscape from an early day, but it was some time before they appreciated that besides great fertility, our land had shore and mountain charm to offer vacationers, before they realized the recreational possibilities in our natural resources.

LAKE SHORE RESORTS

A lake resort called Linden Beach was built about 1870 at the end of Hardy Road on what had been Governor Huntington's farm. A large dining room served the summer residents of the cottage and tent colony. Vacationers took drives along the shore or splashed in the shallow water. In the evening they enjoyed musicales and charades. Linden Beach continued to thrive for twenty-five years.

West of Linden Beach the Shore Club was established on the Lathrop and Smart farms in 1898. A green two-story frame building with large porches was the Club House, center of social events. Several cottages were built and Clevelanders came to occupy bedrooms in the Club House. Painesville families found it a pleasant day's drive and the Shore Club remained a popular holiday attraction until the Diamond Alkali Company bought the property in 1921.

The summer hotel at Salida Beach on Lake Drive, Mentor-on-the-Lake, was flourishing in the Nineties and into the present century. It was a three-story frame building with wide porches on the first and second floors, built and managed as a resort by R. A. Parks. Eventually sold to the Episcopal Church for the use of the Girls' Friendly Society, it was renamed Holiday House.

Mentor Headlands was another lake resort at the turn of the century. A number of big farm houses welcomed summer guests, and the area became well known for good and ample home-cooked food, refreshing breezes and a fine bathing beach.

Willoughbeach Park, opposite the present Shoregate Shopping Center, was the last word in resort pleasure in the first decades of the new century. In addition to bathing and picnicking, pop corn stands and ice cream booths, it had a merry-go-round and dance pavillion, especially popular with the young people of the county.

THE INTERURBAN

The year 1896 brought a great innovation to our residents and to the vacationers. The Cleveland, Painesville & Ashtabula Interurban laid a street car line along Euclid Avenue on the south side of Mentor Avenue to Painesville. Sturdy comfortable passenger cars and baggage cars made good time and ran frequently. Two years later the Shore Line from Cleveland to Willoughby serviced Willoughbeach Park and opened up new areas for summer cottages. The line was eventually extended to Ashtabula and joined the trolley from Buffalo.

The car barns, the original power plant, and the company's offices were at Willoughby and provided work for many. Later, when it purchased its electricity from the Cleveland Electric Illuminating Company, the C. P. & A. introduced electricity to the farmers along its route.

Our Interurban not only brought more holiday seekers, but was very important to the year-round residents of the County. In a Cleveland newspaper in 1909, an article describing a trip to Ashtabula, said, "The whole route was like one village street. . . . The way the people used the trolley, too, made it seem like one long town. Children hopped off and on with their books, men carried tools, shrub sprouts and musical instruments." All along the line there was easy transportation to high school, stores and recreation sites. Until 1926, when the C. P. & A. lost to competition from automobiles, the Interurban was a very real part of our life. "We live at Stop 47," "Turn right at Stop 61" were common expressions long after the last street car had passed.

THE LITTLE MOUNTAIN HOUSE

One of the earliest natural beauty spots to be developed as a recreation area was Little Mountain. Although its peak lies mainly in Geauga County, it has been of importance to Lake County for our pleasure and the business it brought. In 1831 Simeon Reynolds built a large hotel, The Little Mountain House, and operated it successfully until his son John took over the management.

The Reynolds' account book gives a picture of the year 1848. For instance, Mr. C. W. Willey paid $2.50 per week for board. He had brought his horse and another entry shows a charge of 37c for "Boarding Pompey about ten days." From the accounts it is evident that the guests ate unbelievable quantities of food; but the chickens cost the hotel keeper eight and ten cents apiece; butter was ten cents a pound, and eggs six cents a dozen.

In addition to food, lodging, clear bracing air and a wonderful view, the hotel offered recreation. The account book shows that groups bowling were charged 25c a day. It also shows the payments to "Boys Tending Alleys" and "Boys Setting up Pins." They worked many days to earn dollar.

MORE LITTLE MOUNTAIN RESORTS

Little Mountain's fame spread and accommodations for more and more people were provided. In 1850 D. W. Stocking of Chardon built a "colossal" hotel, destined to outlive all the other resort buildings. Serving the public twenty-five years, The Stocking House was sold to a group of Cleveland millionaires to become the Little Mountain Club, finally torn down in 1941.

In 1855 Dr. H. R. Gatchell of Cleveland and Dr. Storm Rosa of Painesville bought twenty-two acres of land directly south of The Little Mountain House. They erected a large bathing house and gymnasium for the treatment of invalids, using what was then popularly known as the water cure. William S. Gardiner became a partner in the venture and he added a boarding house. This was operated for a few years as The Little Mountain Eagle.

In 1868 Charles A. Avery bought The Little Mountain House and changed its name to The Lakeview House. A letter to the *Telegraph* describes life at the resort in those days: "Between sleeping and eating and reading, a part of the boarders wait in untold happiness for Tempus to Fugit. Others ramble in the woods, play games, especially whist, and others anxiously wait for the dinner bell to ring."

Avery prospered. Ten years later he formed the Pine Crest Hotel Company with capital stock of $75,000 to replace his 1831 building.

The brochure printed for the 1900 summer season states; "The guest's chambers are of good size and perfectly ventilated. They are single and en suite, with baths attached, private balconies, open fireplaces, etc. . . . Cottages situated in picturesque rows convenient to Hotel are of various sizes and are all fully furnished and cared for same as rooms in the Hotel. . . . Every amusement possible is provided for the guests. Frequent Hops, with music from an excellent orchestra, Billiards, Bowling Alleys, Concerts and various entertainments. An excellent Livery is maintained, and picturesque drives about the surrounding country are very popular."

LITTLE MOUNTAIN MEMORIES

Even before 1900 the pattern of social life began to change. Former summer visitors, like the Garfields, bought farms. Many people wanted their own summer homes. Others wanted more sophisticated resorts. Eventually the automobile had its effect on the popular vacation spot. The Pine Crest Hotel was dismantled. One by one the cottages were closed and the Club lost its members. Today few houses remain. Little Mountain is private property, no longer open to the public, but still a wonderful conservation of virgin forest and fascinating rock formation.

The attractions of Little Mountain brought many people into the county for a night, a week or a summer. Some grew to love our countryside and when they looked for land for their own summer home, they started their search in our county. One of the early members of this new wave of immigration was George Hopper.

GEORGE H. HOPPER

Hopper had been born in England in 1837, and his father had brought the family to America four years later. George went to school in Cleveland, then learned the cooper's trade. He early showed mechanical skill and business initiative, and won a contract to make barrels for the booming oil industry of the '70's.

His were good barrels, made of white oak staves, well cured in his own kiln. He had a useful product to sell John D. Rockefeller, and his little business grew. But oil was not like other liquids he had handled. It had a way of leaking through the soundest wooden barrel. Rockefeller might not have minded the mess on his warehouse floor, but he certainly did not like the waste, and had so told his supplier.

Sitting on his Cleveland doorstep one evening, Hopper was meditating his problem when a tramp came along and asked for a bite to eat. He was a decent looking fellow and carried himself with dignity for all his shabby clothes. As dusk settled down Hopper found himself telling his troubles to this unlikely confidant. The tramp finished his meal and asked for a paper and pencil. "Try this formula," he said, "and thanks for the meal." He was gone before Hopper had time to decipher the letters.

Next day Hopper mixed the tramp's formula. He skeptically painted a few barrels with it, set them to dry and then filled them with oil. The following morning he found a clean floor around them. His contract was safe, his business assured. Later he sold his company to Rockefeller's Standard Oil and served the rest of his life as director of that company and manager of its cooperage department.

HOPPER COMES TO LAKE COUNTY

About 1880 Hopper bought a large track of land on County Line Road and Middle Ridge in Unionville and became a resident of Lake County. Here he had space to raise the fine horses he loved and found easy transportation on the railroad to his business interests. As his children married, a settlement of spacious homes grew up, a settlement known for its hospitality, not only by its guests from Cleveland and New York, but known as well by every hobo on the road. By Hopper's strict orders no tramp was ever turned from the door. All were fed generously. All were questioned. But no one ever identified the man of the formula. Hopper was never able to reward his benefactor.

COUNTRY ESTATES AND GENTLEMAN FARMERS

George H. Hopper was the forerunner of a large number of Cleveland industrialists who were drawn to Lake County by its beauty and their love of country life. Oil, coal and iron, shipping, railroads and manufacturing built wealth in the city for these men to enjoy spending in our county. They bought land, built large and comfortable summer homes and devoted themselves to raising pedigreed livestock. These gentleman farmers brought city conveniences, improved transportation and luxury goods to our markets.

The first area developed was the ridge in Wickliffe which became by 1895 a ribbon of estates, each beautifully landscaped. These summer residences were not self-supporting, but their owners had means to employ a large labor force. As in Fairport's expansion, there was more work than men available. Perhaps it was Wickliffe's Harry Coulby (in 1916 to become the first mayor of the incorporated village) who brought in a group of Italians to work around his Roman villa, which is now the City Hall. The Italians, a fun-loving people, gracious and hospitable, have added music and color to our pattern of life with their customs and holidays.

As transportation improved the summer residents spread further east to Waite Hill, Mentor and Kirtland. One of these estates is described by

Orville Prescott in his *Five Dollar Gold Piece.* He wrote: "Winden was wonderful, a 200-acre farm in Kirtland. . . . It was a working farm with cows and horses and sheep and poultry, orchards and pastures, fields of oats, alfalfa and corn. Grandfather Sherwin employed a superintendent, a dairyman and a number of farm hands and gardeners to operate it. But his ideas for improvements kept altering its character, making it less and less a working farm and more and more like a country estate.

"He built an aviary where he kept golden pheasants. He installed rustic benches and bridges at convenient locations. He built a new and handsome gate and a new driveway which swept up to the Big House in graceful curves. All of these changes, and the elaborate garden which he did not live to see completed, were expressions of his abiding love of beauty. Usually he did not put his feelings into words, but once as he stood on the veranda at Winden and looked across his own acres and the serene valley of the east branch of the Chagrin River to the Kirtland hills, where a white church spire gleamed, he exclaimed to his niece, 'Ruth, heaven couldn't be more beautiful than this!'"

OUR PARK SYSTEM

More and more vacationers appreciated the recreational possibilities in our natural resources, but to trace the development of our residents' growing appreciation we need to go back to our early days. The idea of town parks came from the New England village green. This open land in the center of the community was at first common pasture where anyone could graze a cow. Most of our Western Reserve towns were laid around this central park, which here became the hub of social as well as business activity.

Later these village greens had band stands and for many years concerts were given one evening a week through the summer. Townspeople gathered under the trees. Small boys darted here and there. Horse and buggies from the country lined the curbs. The porches of nearby houses had all their rockers filled and the cushions on the steps were taken over by the young people. A gay and noisy crowd almost drowned out the loud and rhythmic renditions from drums and brasses.

TOWNSHIP AND MUNICIPAL PARKS

When more and more of the Lake shore became privately owned the first move for public recreation areas started. Everyone had been free to use Hopkins Point for bathing and picnicking. To preserve that privilege, Mentor Township bought a number of these acres in 1899 for a public beach. In 1906 Painesville's Township Park was established some distance west of the present site. Its old pavilion was later used for a few years as company offices by the Diamond Alkali Company.

Today public beaches spread along much of our shore. Painesville Pumping Station, Fairport, North Perry Park, Perry Township Park, Tuttle Park and Madison Township Park are now dwarfed by the large Ohio State Headlands Park, which draws sun and water lovers from all over northeastern Ohio. People escape from the shadows of towering buildings as our forefathers did from their overwhelming forests.

As the towns built up there were no longer handy cow pastures for spontaneous sports. At this time our municipalities bought land for public use. Now Wickliffe's City Hall property, Gilson and Daniels Park in Willoughby, Painesville's Recreation Park and Eastlake's new Reeves Road Park all offer room for games and play. Mentor Recreation Park and Diamond Alkali's Mountain View Club furnish their members with the same opportunities.

THE BURROUGHS CLUB

About 1916 a group of nature lovers contributed a set of the writings of John Burroughs, famed American naturalist, to Willoughby's library. Out of this small beginning grew the pioneer of all our nature and garden clubs, the Burroughs Club. The members welcomed the arrival of Dr. C. M. Shipman who brought his knowledge and enthusiasm to the group. Many Cleveland naturalists attended the meetings and found the programs and company well worth the trip from the city.

The Burroughs Club was the beginning of a new trend in park planning in the County, a movement toward preserving natural beauty spots, places to enjoy nature, places to learn about trees, shrubs, flowers, birds and animals native to our woods. Appropriately, Dr. Shipman's name is remembered in the Shipman Wildlife Park, a piece of Mentor Marsh owned by the State and adjacent to its beach property.

NATURE PARKS

We benefit by Cleveland's early realization of the value of nature preservation, and enjoy her Metropolitan Park in the western end of the county. North Chagrin Reservation has woods, small lakes and creeks, foot trails, bridle paths and automobile roads. Chapin State Forest, on Gildersleeve Mountain south of Kirtland village is another area for hiking and nature study. It is used by the State as an experimental station in forest conservation, and has much the same natural growth and rock formation as Little Mountain. Our Lake County Park Board is now buying land in the hills and valleys as rapidly as it is available and their finances permit.

To further the interest in nature a committee called POGOS has been formed. It works to promote the Preservation Of Green Open

Spaces. A national organization's efforts are also bearing fruit. Nature Conservancy helps local groups acquire untouched land which, deeded to Nature Conservancy, is turned over to a local institution to maintain. The first such property in Lake County, sixty acres of virgin forest just south of the town of Madison, was given in 1962 by Mr. and Mrs. Carl R. Kimball. It will be used by Kent State University for long-range research in the natural sciences. Preserving more of Mentor Marsh in its natural state is a current project of Nature Conservancy.

HOLDEN ARBORETUM

When Albert Fairchild Holden died in Cleveland in 1913, he left a substantial amount of money to found an arboretum. Steps were taken to bring it into being in 1931 through the efforts of his daughter Mrs. Benjamin P. Bole, a resident of Lake County. She and her husband gave land in Kirtland Hills, friends gave land and money, until in 1961 there were seventeen hundred acres with four thousand varieties of trees, shrubs and vines growing there. The largest arboretum in acres in North America, it is on its way to being the finest. Growing not only our native trees but many rare imported plants, Holden Arboretum also owns Stebbins Gulch in Chardon Township. Here many types of flora remain which for the most part retreated thousands of years ago to the near arctic regions. Unusual song birds, rare wild flowers, deer and other wild life are found here, a fascinating place to explore.

For more than a hundred years our Lake shore, our rolling hills and valleys have drawn vacationers to our county. Resorts have flourished and died away. Summer homes have now turned into year-around residences. Today's new nature parks serve our increasing population by making Lake County a pleasanter place to live. They are the modern expression of Our Continuing Resource — the natural beauty of our countryside.

Chapter XVI

The Twentieth Century

The first decade of the Twentieth Century was a comfortable one in Lake County. Farmers prospered. Bit by bit conveniences came into their lives and isolation vanished. In the Lake County Historical Society Library are memoirs of Virginia A. Billings including excerpts from her mother's letters to her while Virginia was a missionary in Turkey. They tell of life in Kirtland about 1905, typical for all the County.

TURN OF THE CENTURY

"As the time drew near when the children were grown up and no longer attended Peck's Corners school it became a moot question of how they were to get the mail. . . . It was a two mile walk from our house to the office and back. Fortunately about this time the Free Rural Delivery system was established to the great joy of the whole countryside, and Father and Mother then thought they 'lived right in town.'

"Another great convenience was brought to them . . . when the Kirtland telephone was installed. . . . [Mother wrote], 'There are five phones on this street now . . . but five are enough on this wire. Our neighbors are all very socially inclined and they keep the calls going very lively. . . . It makes life more social and really promotes a very friendly feeling in this neighborhood.'

"For several years Father milked five or six Jersey cows and strained the milk into large crocks kept in the pantry until the cream had raised, then Mother skimmed it and Father churned it in a big barrel churn. . . . In one of her letters Mother wrote, 'The only thing of importance that has transpired since my last is the setting up of the new separator, and the trials and vexations we have endured with it. . . . It is quite ornamental, has a very fine cerulean blue frame work with very bright and shiny trimmings . . . and really brightens up our old dingy wood house quite a bit, but the workings of the thing are something that tries ones soul and temper.' A week later she wrote, 'I thought . . . the separator was going to make my life miserable, but as time goes on it assumes less formidable features. I guess in time I shall like it as well as the other way, and Papa takes so much pleasure in grinding out the cream that I feel more willing to put up with it. . . . Men are so fond of machinery.'

"The advent of the automobile was at first a great trial to most country folk. . . . In June 1905 Mother wrote, 'Automobiles are plentiful this season. A frightful looking one, so large and bright red went sailing up the other street (Chillicothe Road half a mile away) and must have gone over twenty miles an hour, the limit for country riding, but we are helpless. . . . I wish . . . [the horses] were not so afraid of automobiles as I suppose we will meet them at every turn this summer. . . . There have not been many about yet, but the roads are being scraped and I presume they will soon be tearing up and down the land.' "

WILSON'S OF WILLOUGHBY

Used by the Billings and many another family was the Sidney S. Wilson Co. of Willoughby. "Everything from Little Wooden Toothpicks to Heavy Lumber Wagons" was its justifiable boast. The store spread along the west side of Erie Street very nearly from Glenn to Spaulding, 18,000 square feet of floor space. It sold "Dry Goods, Carpets, Draperies, Millinery, Men's Furnishings, Shoes, Books, Groceries and Vehicles."

The Grocery Department carried almost entirely packaged goods. Going were the days when flour, sugar, cracker, pickle, salt pork and molasses barrels crowded the floor space, and walls were lined with hoppers filled with rolled oats, beans, tea, spices and dried fruits. Modern merchandising had begun. From the small store inherited by Sidney V. Wilson from his father-in-law, Samuel Smart, the next generation of Sidney S. Wilson saw it grow to be the largest country store between New York and Chicago.

NEW TRENDS IN INDUSTRY

While Lake County farmers were enjoying improved equipment in their homes and stores, other men were also feeling the impact of labor saving devices. In 1901 the Cleveland Crane & Engineering Company built a plant near the village of Wickliffe to manufacture overhead cranes used to move heavy equipment. This was one of the steps toward our modern production line of manufacturing. As Cleveland Crane expanded, more and more of our citizens learned the factory way of life.

Labor saving machinery brought automation to Fairport in 1906 when car-dumping equipment was installed at the docks and manual labor was no longer needed to fill the boats with coal. Steam shovels already had replaced hand shoveling to remove the ore. Machines, together with the national financial panic of 1907, threatened to turn Fairport into a ghost town again. The answer came in the growth of new industry in the county.

A waiting labor force and a hitherto untapped mineral resource, the great salt beds which lie deep along the Lake shore, attracted the first of our chemical companies, Diamond Alkali. In 1911 construction of the factory was begun and with it began our part in the Twentieth Century Chemical Age.

MANAGEMENT AND WORKERS

Back breaking physical labor was passing for both farmer and industrial worker. Small plants were being replaced by large mechanized factories. Owner operation was giving way to management control. An indication of management's attitude toward the worker at this time can be gathered from the following Cleveland Crane advertisement published in *Lake County Illustrated* in 1912.

"This Company as an institution for the social-industrial betterment in the community is accomplishing many things and it is with pleasure that we point to the generous policy being employed.

"Their custom of taking on apprentices, starting them in the shop and following their progress through the organization, into the high executive positions, makes it easy for every Lake County parent to know what to do with his boy's career.

"The Cleveland Crane & Engineering Co. is also on the lookout at all times for good men and their progress is of their own shaping. To stimulate the element of thrift with its employees this company has opened an allotment in Wickliffe, where the employee may purchase a home at a reasonable price and a small down payment. Already many homes have been built."

Cleveland Crane also had a bonus system for their workers and sponsored a band for the enjoyment of the community. A new concept, employer-employee relations, was entering the industrial picture.

THE MOTORING AGE

In the fall of 1913 A. R. Marsh started a factory in Painesville to build automobiles. The following year the Vulcan, "The World's Greatest Light Car," was on the market.

"Thousands of dealers and prospective owners have been waiting for the right car at the right price. . . . Others have hit all around the mark, but the Vulcan is the first to hit the Bull's eye. . . . Will climb any hill where the wheels will hold, and stand the severest tests to which a motor can be subjected. . . . A car with no objectionable features. . . . In addition to our present large factories, we are prepared to invest millions in additional capacity. . . . The Vulcan is not of 'Mushroom Growth,' years have been spent in the perfection of the car and equipping to manufacture in large quantities."

Orders poured in, but unfortunately, "the millions" were not forth-
coming.   Inefficiency and poor management finished the story.   The
company went into bankruptcy in 1915.   The engineers worked for another year in Painesville as the Erie Car Company before they left Lake
County.

The Vulcan had a short life, but long enough for a number of teen-
agers to become the envy of their friends.   These boys were the test driv-
ers, working from 7 A. M. to 5 P. M. all summer, testing the perform-
ance of chassis.   Favorite obstacles were Hogsback Hill in Concord Township and Main Street hill in Painesville.   The touring car's top speed was
37 miles per hour when all was in good condition.   Who would think of
test driving as work?   Not the boys of 1914!

Of even briefer fame was the Ben Hur car.   A factory was built in
Willoughby and one car made for demonstration.   Its name might be
forgotten if the building had not been put to dramatic use a few years
later.

Cars were first a sporting matter, a novelty, then gradually became a
convenience.   About 1918 the County Commissioners felt the pressure
of modern life sufficiently to allow the County Engineer the time-saving
device of using a taxi when he had any extensive trip to crowd into a day.
So one fine morning the Engineer and his assistant started off in a model
T Ford with a greenhorn from the city at the wheel.   They inspected
ditches and culverts in Concord and Leroy and in the late afternoon
started for home.   The driver had about all the scenery he needed and all
the bumpy, dusty roads.   He lit out for Painesville.

The car was going at a good clip when it arrived at the top of Blair
Hill.   It slithered down around one curve after another, scarcely slowing,
bumping from one rut to the next.   The two men in the back seat clutched
their straw hats with one hand and with the other clung to any bracket
they could reach.   Suddenly, the driver slammed on the brakes and
skidded to a shivering halt on the clanking boards of the covered bridge.
"Whew!" said our hero, mopping his brow, "It certainly was lucky them
barn doors was open!"

The problems which Mrs. Billings described with her horses and passing cars continued for some years, not only for the farmer, but for the
motorist as well.   It was no joke to meet a team on a narrow, rutted hill
and cope with hand brake and gear shift.   Gradually roads were widened,
some were even paved.   Carriage horses were put to pasture and the motorist was king.

WORLD WAR I

This peaceful and uncomplicated life in Lake County was interrupted
by World War I.   Children hunted chores to earn money for Thrift

Stamps. Parents put all they could spare into War Bonds. All shared Meatless Tuesdays and Wheatless Wednesdays. Housewives brought out their grandmother's recipes for cornmeal cakes to save precious white flour, scarce because every available pound was sent to Europe for our Allies.

In one window after another service flags began to appear, a star for each soldier who had gone from that home, twenty-six to be replaced before the war was over by a gold star, meaning a life had been given.

Coal was scarce. Sugar was scarce. Every one, very nearly, had a Victory Garden. Front lawns were plowed up. Flower gardens were planted with beans, cabbages and tomatoes. In the manpower shortage farmerettes in khaki knickers appeared and many a farmer found these city girls could do a good day's work.

The Red Cross called women into groups to roll bandages and they knitted day and night. Experts could even produce a few inches while watching a movie. Life speeded up for everyone.

LEWISITE GAS

Lake County's most dramatic part in World War I took place in the former Ben Hur plant in Willoughby. Here a thousand soldiers, mostly trained chemists, made a highly dangerous methyl gas. It was the most deadly chemical to have been developed at that time. Gas masks were no protection because the poison entered the blood immediately, penetrating skin and clothing.

In a plant surrounded by barbed wire, the men worked in great secrecy. They were not allowed to mention Willoughby in their letters, and all their mail went through a post office box in Cleveland. At first the men were not allowed to leave the grounds, except under guard, but this provision was later modified. Denied even the occasional rest and recreation given to a fighting soldier, without the stimulus of actual battle, these men labored for months under a threat of death more terrible than if they had been in the front line trenches. They were truly heroes.

The gas was to have been used in the spring of 1919 in a bombardment from the Alps to the English Channel. The German Army was saved by the Armistice, and the tons of Lewisite were carefully convoyed by train to the Atlantic, gingerly transferred to barges and dumped far out at sea, instead of on the enemy.

THE TWENTIES

The Armistice began a decade of quiet expansion for Lake County. Diamond Alkali increased its variety of products. Industrial Rayon opened a plant in Painesville Township. Ohio Rubber took over the Lewisite plant. More and more of our citizens became industrial workers.

Agriculture was still profitable and fruit remained an important crop. Nurseries grew and an occasional tractor could be seen in the fields. Electricity reached farther and farther into the country. Automobiles became common and more roads were paved. The Interurban went out of business, but the Accomodation train still ran to Cleveland in the morning and back at night with frequent stops.

State legislation lengthened compulsory school attendance age from six to eighteen. The law also instructed rural districts to pay tuition and provide transportation to nearby high schools, or to build their own schools. Our modern network of public schools was finally on its way.

Andrews School for Girls moved to its new campus. The boarding school had been planned by Mr. and Mrs. Wallace C. Andrews to give vocational secondary education at a nominal cost. This was particularly advantageous to country girls who could not easily get to town high schools. Now this need was taken care of by the new state law, and Andrews had an opportunity to expand and broaden its objectives.

The Twenties were the heyday of the summer people. Waite Hill Village was incorporated, as was Kirtland Hills. On the Lake, Mentor Harbor Yacht Club was developed. Mentor Headlands Golf and Tennis Club flourished in a cluster of summer cottages. Madison Golf Lakelands was laid out. The former Everett estate became the Kirtland Country Club. Golf courses, private and public, were developed in every community. Lake County farmers could sell any land which was at all scenic to the rush of city people. There was a fine feeling of prosperity.

THE DEPRESSION YEARS

This prosperity of the Twenties ended abruptly at the close of the decade, here as well as across the country. The stock market crash was followed by increasingly difficult years. Ohio Rubber, largely dependent on the automobile industry, was hard hit. Cleveland Crane's fine machinery was in little or no demand. Diamond Alkali, with greater diversification, was able to spread its work somewhat. Lubrizol struggled through its first years in Wickliffe.

Lowering food prices meant less income for the farmers. Some were caught with loans for modern equipment and lost their farms as a result. A Farm and Home Protection Committee examined loan foreclosures and was able to help many. The Thirties, however, brought one forward step in agriculture. Clumsy tractors were trimmed down and put on rubber tires. This was a big advance in their usability and marked the end of horse power on the farms.

Retail trade in vegetables and fruit was probably as good a business as there was in the county through the first half of the 1930's. General unemployment prevailed. Everyone was affected. Two generations moved in together and pinched their pennies in every possible way. Back-yard gardens again helped stretch food budgets.

Our County relief resources were nearly exhausted when the national Works Project Administration stepped in. The first project to get under way was road work. Men found jobs grading, ditching, repaving. Then schools were renovated and playgrounds constructed. Fairport gained a library building. A mattress factory there and a sewing center in Paines-ville gave work to others. Somehow or other we lived through these rugged years until the war in Europe and the demand for goods it brought, began to put the industrial world back on its feet. The Depression had made us more aware that what happened outside the County made a dif-ference to us too.

RISE OF THE UNIONS

The most important development of the Thirties was undoubtedly the organization of labor unions. Railroad workers and the building trades had had their craft unions long before this, and there were well estab-lished American Federation of Labor locals here. But the factory work-ers had no unions. It was a long hard struggle before the Congress of Industrial Organizations was accepted in 1936 at Ohio Rubber and in 1941 by Diamond Alkali and Industrial Rayon. It was not only man-agement's position which caused the delay, but it was also the individual-ism of many of the workers who hesitated to join this group activity. The union leaders persisted, and while the first ten years were difficult for everyone, by 1960 a working relationship between management and labor was established. Ninety-five percent of the county's working force is now organized, divided between United Mine Workers and AFL-CIO. The union leaders feel they have brought stability to their communities, better working conditions for their members and, above all, given every man the dignity in labor which should be his.

WORLD WAR II

The second World War brought many more hardships to our citizens than had the first. Factories all over the country converted to war pro-duction. Consumers' goods ran short. Autos, washing machines and stoves were unobtainable except rarely at secondhand. Tires, gasoline, shoes and food were rationed. Everyone worked. Women took jobs never before open to them.

The war illuminated the changes in our eating habits that had oc-curred in the twenty-five years since World War I. White flour was available, but meat, butter, sugar and most canned foods were rationed. Every household again canned vegetables and fruit. A few families, fortunate to have the new household freezers, were able to save every bit of surplus yield from their gardens. "Vitamins for Victory" was the ringing homefront cry of World War II.

More of the self-sufficiency of Lake County disappeared as we shared the same privations, the same inconveniences, as the rest of the country. The problems of the world were on our doorstep. Traditional isolationism of the Middle West disappeared as our boys fought on many shores. They came back with an awareness of foreign affairs (and often with British, French, German or Japanese brides) — an awareness which could not help but enlarge our vision.

SUBURBIA

From the days of the Depression more and more of the summer cottages had been converted into year-around homes. People did not forget the value of a little garden space, learned through the lean years. All over the country city people had a resurgence of nostalgia for the farms of their grandfathers. More and more wanted to have a little open land around them, to leave behind the heat, grime and hubbub of city streets. Lake County offered space and natural beauty in contrast to cosmopolitan Cleveland. Our population boomed. Census figures rose fifty percent from 1940 to 1950, doubled in the next decade.

Houses sprang up almost over night. School Boards struggled to keep up with the ever increasing demand for new buildings and more teachers. Shopping centers moved in with the population and prospered where only a few years before there would not have been enough people in a five mile radius to support them. New industries spread along the railroads, many of them as beautifully landscaped as the finest homes. Now new roads are cutting across the country to bring more and more people to and through Lake County.

With all the expansion of industry and home sites, agriculture is still an important part of our economy. There are many farms in the eastern and southern parts of the county, and there are nurseries everywhere. In the decade after 1950 the number of nurseries doubled and the acres in nursery crops increased fifty percent. They not only bring a good living to many, but they add to our pleasant landscape.

The postwar era has brought with its increasing population a tremendous number and variety of new churches. The older churches have enlarged their facilities also. Libraries have grown and new branches have been opened. Lake Erie College offers a School of Community Education for teacher preparation. It also runs an off-campus College Center as a Junior College in Painesville. The Chandler Technical School, under the supervision of the Ohio State Board of Education, enrolled its first students in the fall of 1962 in Willoughby. Borromeo Seminary and

Telshe Yeshiva, both in Wickliffe, both accredited colleges, offer training for the priesthood or rabbinate. Our cultural life keeps pace with our population.

OUR DEVELOPMENT

There have been two primary forces in our development from virgin forest to the Lake County of the Sixties — our natural resources and the men who have lived here. Climate and fertility made prosperous farms and still support farms and nurseries. Climate and beauty have brought us a continuing stream of vacationers, summer residents and new full-time citizens. Natural sources of water power and iron ore deposits started our industry. Our water supply and underground salt deposits drew new companies, and in today's chemical age, will probably continue to do so.

But people have the most influence on what kind of community develops. The early pioneers were nearly all from the same background. This common heritage gave social solidity. Goals for government, education and religion were much the same for everyone. Standards for work, thrift and initiative were alike, and recreation was healthy. Each new group has added its flavor and variety to the basic philosophy of our society; even the suburban inundation has not changed it.

Important too, has been the fact that men of influence in the county have been fine men and good citizens, generous of their time and effort. While some left to make their fortunes in urban centers, many men of culture remained, found satisfactory means of support, and worked to make a good society. No one produced phenomenal wealth, but these men have had intelligence, integrity and enterprise, a sense of justice and decency, and the courage to meet new ideas and new people.

May we follow in their footsteps, avoiding dangerous extremes, respecting the old, welcoming the new. For what we do today and tomorrow is the future history of Lake County.

INDEX

CENSUS RECORD OF LAKE COUNTY

There are no complete census records before 1820 for Ohio. In 1802, Painesville Township which included Chardon, Hampden, Montville, Leroy, Concord, Perry, Mentor and Kirtland had 83 men of voting age. In 1810, Painesville Township included Concord, Perry, Mentor and Kirtland. It was the sixth largest population center on the Reserve with 670 residents. In 1820, Painesville Township, including Concord, was the largest community of the Reserve.

TOTALS BY TOWNSHIPS AND VILLAGES
1820 - 1960

	1820	1830	1840	1850	1860	1870	1880	1890	1900	1910	1920	1930	1940	1950*	1960*
Concord Twp.		979	1,136	1,031	953	797	722	601	706	608	623	710	795	1,440	3,860
Kirtland Twp. incl. parts of	481	1,018	1,778	1,598	1,231	1,029	984	909	1,134	1,047	957	1,602	1,859	2,663	4,709
Kirtland Hills												(206)	(237)	(235)	(292)
Waite Hill												(237)	(289)	(305)	(360)
Leroy Twp.	125	652	898	1,128	884	811	722	632	678	664	693	683	827	937	1,502
Madison Twp. incl.	948	1,898	2,800	2,986	3,030	2,913	2,720	2,630	2,720	2,876	2,885	3,267	3,704	5,018	9,841
Madison Village					(558)	(757)	(793)	(738)	(768)	(863)	(893)	(927)	(979)	(1,127)	(1,347)
Mentor Twp. incl.	460	703	1,245	1,571	1,613	1,666	1,822	1,650	1,835	1,977	2,112	3,772	5,263	9,905	24,942
Mentor Village						(416)	(540)	(502)	(624)	(732)	(851)	(1,589)	(1,827)	(2,383)	(4,354)
Mentor-on-the-Lake												(230)	(538)	(1,413)	(3,290)
Painesville Twp. incl.	1,278	1,499	2,580	3,128	4,388	4,995	5,516	7,558	9,282	9,601	14,019	18,673	20,472	25,501	27,997
Fairport Harbor									(2,073)	(2,263)	(4,211)	(4,972)	(4,528)	(4,519)	(4,267)
Grand River									(332)	(203)	(248)	(314)	(305)	(448)	(477)
Painesville City					(2,676)	(3,728)	(3,841)	(4,755)	(5,024)	(5,501)	(7,272)	(10,944)	(12,235)	(14,432)	(12,967)
Perry Twp. incl.	626	1,148	1,339	1,131	1,174	1,208	1,316	1,365	1,687	1,784	1,693	2,072	2,313	2,974	4,834
North Perry												(316)	(318)	(470)	(658)
Perry Village											(473)	(602)	(615)	(665)	(885)
Willoughby Twp. incl.	752	1,277	1,943	2,081	2,308	2,516	2,524	2,890	3,638	4,370	5,685	10,895	14,787	27,541	67,214
Eastlake														(7,486)	(12,467)
Lakeline													(77)	(183)	(269)
Timberlake														(236)	(670)
Wickliffe											(1,508)	(2,491)	(3,155)	(5,002)	(15,760)
Willoughby Village					(587)	(867)	(1,001)	(1,219)	(1,753)	(2,072)		(4,045)	(4,345)	(5,450)	(15,058)
Willoughby Hills															(4,241)
Willowick												(667)	(915)	(3,677)	(18,749)
LAKE COUNTY TOTAL	4,670	9,174	13,719	14,654	15,581	15,935	16,326	18,235	21,680	22,927	28,667	41,674	50,020	75,979	148,700

* These figures vary slightly because incorporation lines overlap old Township lines.

LAKE COUNTY POPUL

BY COMMUNITY AND CEN

APRIL 1960

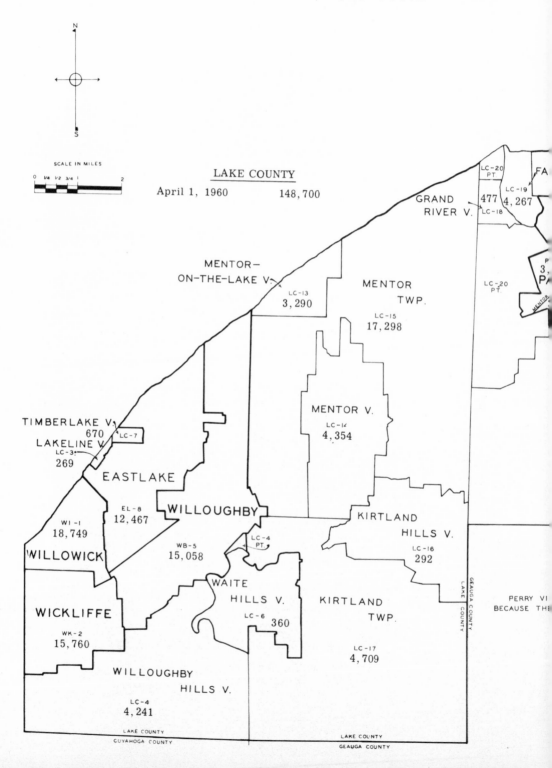

N

S

SCALE IN MILES

0 1/4 1/2 3/4 1   2

LAKE COUNTY

April 1, 1960   148,700

LC-20
PT.   FA

LC-19
477 4,267

GRAND
RIVER V.   LC-18

MENTOR—
ON-THE-LAKE V.

MENTOR
TWP.

LC-20
PT.   P
3,
PA

LC-13
3,290

LC-15
17,298

MENTOR V.
LC-14
4,354

TIMBERLAKE V.
670   LC-7

LAKELINE V.
LC-3
269

EASTLAKE

EL-8
12,467   WILLOUGHBY

WI-1
18,749

KIRTLAND
HILLS V.

LC-16
292

WILLOWICK

WB-5
15,058

LC-4
PT.

WAITE
HILLS V.

LC-6 360

KIRTLAND
TWP.

GEAUGA COUNTY
LAKE COUNTY

PERRY VI
BECAUSE THE

WICKLIFFE

WK-2
15,760

WILLOUGHBY
HILLS V.

LC-4
4,241

LC-17
4,709

LAKE COUNTY
CUYAHOGA COUNTY

LAKE COUNTY
GEAUGA COUNTY